# PASSIVE INCOME

## QUICK START PLAYBOOK

## 2 BOOKS IN 1

BEGINNER'S GUIDE FOR FINANCIAL FREEDOM WITH IDEAS AND STRATEGIES ON HOW TO BUILD A DROPSHIPPING E-COMMERCE BUSINESS MODEL AND LONG-DISTANCE REAL ESTATE INVESTING

REAL ESTATE INVESTING FOR BEGINNERS

A FINANCIAL FREEDOM STEP BY STEP GUIDE WITH THE LATEST LOOPHOLES ON HOW TO MAKE MONEY, INVEST, AND CREATE A PASSIVE INCOME CASH FLOW IN THE LONG-DISTANCE

BRANDON J. SWING

DROPSHIPPING SHOPIFY E-COMMERCE

BUSINESS MODEL

THE ULTIMATE STEP BY STEP BEGINNERS GUIDE ON HOW TO CREATE A PASSIVE INCOME CASH FLOW, MAKE MONEY ONLINE FROM HOME AND ACHIEVE FINANCIAL FREEDOM

BRANDON J. SWING

# BRANDON J. SWING

# PASSIVE INCOME QUICK START PLAYBOOK

*Beginner's guide for financial freedom with ideas and strategies on how to build a dropshipping ecommerce business model and long-distance real estate investing*

*2 books in 1*

# REAL ESTATE INVESTING FOR BEGINNERS

*A Financial Freedom Step-By-Step Guide with the Latest Loopholes on How to Make Money, Invest, and Create a Passive Income Cash Flow in the Long-Distance*

## Dropshipping Shopify E-Commerce Business Model

*The Ultimate Step by Step Guide on How to Create a Passive Income Cash Flow, Make Money Online from Home and Achieve Financial Freedom*

*Brandon J. Swing*

# REAL ESTATE INVESTING FOR BEGINNERS

*A Financial Freedom Step-By-Step Guide with the Latest Loopholes on How to Make Money, Invest, and Create a Passive Income Cash Flow in the Long-Distance*

# Table of Contents

**Introduction**

If you want to become a real estate investor, then this book on how to get into real estate investing is right for you.

Becoming successful in real estate investing isn't an easy path. However, this book will help you take the first step by teaching you all the different ways you must follow to become a successful real estate investor. We will cover every detail that a beginner investor might require when getting started, such as tools for real estate investors, education, different real estate strategies, and more.

We all want to control our destiny, work for ourselves, and feel good about making a difference in the world. Real estate investing is a great way to grow one's entrepreneurial muscles.

To help you out in your race to become a real estate entrepreneur, keep reading this book, which breaks down all the necessary information that beginners need to master step by step. So, pay attention and concentrate on everything we have to say about how to master the art of real estate investing.

## Chapter 1: Introduction and How to Find Rental Properties

Have you reached a point in your life where you know you need to do something to boost your retirement income, or you want to find a way to double your spending cash?

This chapter will provide the best foundation to help you find profitable investment properties.

When you invest in real estate, you must be prepared to search for investment properties. That is why this chapter will address the question, "How to find rental properties for sale?" So, just keep on reading.

Real estate investing is making money through rental properties. It may be land, land development, or properties. The thing that makes real estate the best money-making business is the variety of investment methods. There are so many lucrative ways on how to invest in real estate. For that reason, beginner real estate investors will not have any issues getting into this type of business. They can decide to invest in rental properties, which is the easiest investment plan for them. Later on, once they attain the necessary experience, they get to improve their investment levels.

Investing in rental property can be the best move, particularly in the US market, which is strong and growing. If you are planning to invest successfully, you need to make smart choices about what you purchase, where you buy it, and how you organize the acquisition. It's easy to make mistakes, even for experienced investors who have an extensive portfolio of real estate assets.

Don't forget that the decisions you make today will determine how you maintain the property tomorrow. If you are still in the buying process or you have started looking around at prospective investments, you have time to implement plans that will lead to a profitable and successful experience for you. Make decisions that will limit your vacancy, boost your rental income, and attract the best tenants to your rental property.

Your target, as a real estate investor, is to buy a property that will generate a lot of applications quickly so you can get a tenant in place immediately you list the home. This is the best way to optimize your rental income and long-term ROI.

That aside, there are main factors you need to consider when you are getting ready to invest in rental property, and these are as follows:

**Location:** Location is critical in your rental property investment. As an investor, look for an area with a low vacancy rate and where the value of rent appreciates. These areas will generate a huge return on your investment. You will have a few problems making cash flow, and you don't have to worry about generating rental income.

Local expertise is especially crucial when you are considering location and choosing where to invest. You require a property manager who can advise you what each neighborhood is like, the kinds of tenants in place, and whether there is a high turnover. Tenant turnover is costly for investors. If you change tenants every year, you will spend a lot of money improving the home for someone new, marketing the property, and waiting for someone to enter so you can begin collecting rent again.

The best location for a rental property is a developed neighborhood that's a good mix of owner homes and rental properties. You want to buy in a place where people will stay, or where rental values are appreciating. It's not wise to invest in an area where rental rates have been declining. Even if you get the best property and invest a lot of cash into upgrades and updates, you're still in a neighborhood with low rents.

Discuss with your property manager about the demographics and data that determines the neighborhood you're thinking about investing in. You can assess average rental rates and length of residence. Keep in mind that's the market that will determine how much you can charge in rent. It doesn't matter how much you value your home, and it doesn't matter how much you want to collect to break even with your mortgage and other expenses. The rental amount depends on the demand of the market, and a significant part of your market influence emerges from your location.

The location factor includes different things such as transportation, commuter routes, recreation, and the availability of shopping, grocery stores, etc. Find out the quality of the schools before you proceed to buy a property. Families with children going to school will be searching for a good place to send their children. You can discuss the well-rated schools with prospective tenants when they come to see the property.

Public transport is also vital. Neighborhoods that one can walk are increasingly in high demand, especially among millennials. Quality residents are always searching for homes that make their lives easier and enjoyable.

**Investment properties vs. living homes:** Anyone can buy a real estate property. However, not all real estate properties are for investment reasons. When you purchase real estate for sale as an investor, your objective is to keep generating money out of it no matter the strategy. At the same time, when an individual buys a home, his/her target is to live in it. This is where the calculations start. The computations, in this case, are the property valuation methods. These involve investment property analysis and real estate market analysis. These methods are applied in real estate investments to determine the profitability of the property and the place in which it is located. These calculations are not necessary when you purchase a home to live in.

**Finding rental properties through real estate agents:** While real estate agents help those in the market to buy or sell a home, some can also be great resources for serving renters with their dream condos, apartments, and rental homes.

Hiring a real estate agent in a highly competitive market such as Chicago, Los Angeles, and New York can provide a renter with a big advantage in his or her search. Besides listings that can easily be found with simple internet searches, these agents also access listings in the multiple listing service (MLS) database and unlisted units emerging in the market.

Another way real estate agents could benefit you is connections. As you already know, the rental property business is a people's business. As such, you cannot go far without connections. A successful real estate agent has worked with many investors and other agents before. So, he/she is meant to help you find investment properties for sale.

However, remember that you need to look for a real estate agent who is experienced in investment properties. Some agents have only worked with regular homes, and that is a different story. It requires experts to deal with investment properties. Investment deals require real estate investment property analysis. Based on it, you will determine the return on an investment property and identify a profitable one.

If you are interested in improving properties, then including a real estate agent in your team is also a powerful way to find the best investment property. In particular, you want to look for an agent who is specialized in REO properties–properties that are held by a lender because of a defaulted loan. Many lenders align themselves with real estate agents that focus on selling these kinds of properties.

Typically, a real estate agent will help you:

- Locate an investment property for sale that suits your needs and criteria.
- Deliver an accurate estimation of the property's worth.
- Submit and negotiate the offer to the seller's agent on your behalf.
- Having the contract and other documents ready and reviewed.

In general, working with an agent is the most traditional method for beginner property investors to locate houses for sale–regardless of your investment strategy. Remember, however, that for real estate agents to do their job properly, you need to be clear about what you are searching for. So, tell your agent about the type of property you want to invest in, your budget for purchasing a property, your investment goals, etc.

## How to Find Rental Properties Through Networking

You can also find rental properties through networking. This method is not known to everyone, and hence you can purchase a house at a lower value. Relevant networking groups include:

**Personal investor network:** This is a database that features property investors that you have been meeting over the period you have invested in real estate. It might contain other landlords who own real estate properties in the same neighborhood as you or members who happen to be a real estate investor.
**Investment clubs/forums:** These have become popular in the last several years.

They're significant because there is an email list where members share information about real estate properties for sale. They also provide networking opportunities and education that could be important when searching for the right investment property. If you are not a member of any, it might be a good thing to join one.

**Personal friends:** People in the real estate sector aren't the only ones who can introduce you to a good investment opportunity. Family, professional contacts, and friends can be quality resources to identify a rental property for sale.

## How to Find Rental Properties Through Auctions

Real estate auctions are great places for locating houses for sale at discount prices. But, these are interesting methods to find investment properties for real estate investors who have the potential to pay cash for the investment property. There are different types of auctions, including:

- Online auctions
- Sherriff sale auctions
- Private auction companies

Many auction lists are made to the public early before the sales. So, if you analyze these lists, a real estate investor will have the chance to get the best investment property before the sale date. While you can see the property, you might not inspect it or ask for an appraisal before closing.

Purchasing an investment property at an auction has the risk of being taken with a higher bidder. Also, auctioneers will need you to pay 10% of the purchase price down at the time of a winning bid. If you fail to settle within 30 days of the auction, you lose your deposit. Auctions can be a great place to find profitable rental properties for sale.

## Finding Rental Properties Using Print Media

Print media is a powerful way to search for local listings. Some of these properties may not be marketed online, so you will not have stiff competition for them.

**Newspapers:** Newspapers are an excellent source to find 'for sale by owner' properties as well as realtor outlined properties. Make sure to search the main newspaper for your favorite region, plus smaller community newspapers that are focused on specific cities.

**Local marketing publications:** You can get these smaller publications in most grocery stores. They are also a great place to search for properties.

## Other Places to Find Rental Properties

**Craigslist:** Searching for rental property on Craigslist is a simple process. After you decide where you want to invest and the kind of amenities you want in a rental property, use search filters on Craigslist and start to review ads. Don't provide personal information or money to a Craigslist landlord before you meet him or her in person and check the property. Some scammers pretend to be landlords requesting respondents to buy a credit check, complete a rental application, or even pay a deposit before the respondent has even had an opportunity to see the property. The scammer will either disappear with the cash or steal the identity of the respondents.

**Chapter 2: Becoming an Investor**

Real estate investing can generate big profits and allow you to expand your net worth. Despite its huge financial returns, becoming a real estate investor can appear like an intimidating thing to some people. But, with the right knowledge and tools, anyone can do it.

**How to Go About Real Estate Investing**

There are some basic things you need to know before you get started. Below are useful tips to become a real estate investor:

**Get an education.** The first thing to becoming a real estate investor is to acquire sufficient knowledge of the real estate business. As a first-time real estate investor, you must learn about the real estate market, the act of negotiation, and all the details required in purchasing, fixing, and renting out a house.

For example, if you plan to invest in rental properties, you will need to understand the laws and even the average rents for the area. You should also master the risks involved in becoming a real estate investor. Every form of real estate deal may have various risks. In other words, before you purchase your first investment property, you need to ensure that you know everything about the business.

Education doesn't imply getting a four-year degree. You can talk to real estate agents or mentors about different features of the business.

**Choose a niche to get started.** With different niches to select from, becoming a real estate investor may be a little confusing. It can be tiresome if you attempt to jump into many different forms of investment properties. With this confusion, you are likely to make wrong decisions.

It would be better to get started with a single niche. For example, you may choose to go for a wholesaling, residential, commercial, or even flipping real estate. After you master one niche, you can then start a different one. It is hard to specialize in everything at once.

**Develop a business plan.** Like any other investment career, creating a business plan is an important step in becoming a real estate investor. You should take real estate investing as a business and not a hobby. Set your investment goals and how you want to achieve them.

For example, if you decide to buy a distressed property for flipping, your plan should include the market you want to buy in and why, your limits of acquisition expenses, budgets for rehabilitation, and your target sales prices with a time limit for each.

Once you write your business plan, you can share it with your mentor and make any relevant changes.

**Protect your real estate financing.** Becoming a real estate investor is impossible if you don't have funding. Real estate financing is always a big concern for a first-time real estate investor, particularly if they don't have cash.

But, it is impossible to get financing if you know where to find one. There are different options available, such as owner-occupied loans, mortgage loans, private money loans, and hard money loans. You can also choose to partner with investors that are more experienced and have funding but lack time to implement a new property investment.

You should ensure that you improve your credit score and try to build good relationships with lenders. Besides a great credit score, lenders normally want a down payment of at least 20%.

**Network.** Real estate is a people business; you should get out there and meet with professionals and other real estate investors. Strive to create a team that will help you in your journey of becoming a real estate investor. You should get them on board before you invest so that they can help you during the process. Some of the most critical contacts you will need may include real estate agents, contractors, attorneys, lenders, and property managers.

The kind of individuals you will need will depend on your business plan. What they provide should be in line with what you want. For example, you should employ a real estate agent that is an expert working with real estate investors and not homeowners. You can get these contacts by requesting referrals from other successful real estate investors.

**Look for the best real estate deals.** Becoming a real estate investor also demands that you know how to purchase an investment property. But, not every investment property for sale will generate positive cash flow. Therefore, there are some things you should do when you purchase an investment property if you want to be successful. To find the best income properties, make sure you conduct real estate market analysis and rental property investment analysis.

Real estate market analysis will allow you to study the local housing market. Buying a rental property in a great location is important to succeed as a real estate investor. Investing in the best neighborhoods will ensure that your property has the highest tenancy rate because there will be prospective tenants. The best location will also offer more opportunity for appreciation.

On the flip side, investment property analysis will allow you to select the best rental property by computing performance measurements of different investment properties.

**Advantages of Investing in Real Estate**

Every type of investment has its advantages and disadvantages. However, millions know that real estate is the best form of investment as the advantages defeat the disadvantages. If you are thinking about whether you should diversify your investment portfolio with different real estate properties, here are advantages that real estate offers over other types of investment:

- **Diverse choices.** One of the key benefits of real estate investing is the limitless opportunities that it delivers. You can choose from various options, different approaches, different types of properties, different rental strategies, and the list goes on. No matter how much capital you have, what profit on investment you expect, and how active you want to be with your investment. Real estate has the right answer to your needs and expectations.
- **A minimum level of education required.** You don't need to have a degree to enter the real estate investing business. Additionally, thousands of online resources will help you to expand your knowledge as you go. Of course, the real estate business is much of a learning-by-doing business, so you are sure to expand your knowledge base and boost your performance over time.
- **Tangible assets.** Real estate properties are physical properties that you can see and touch. In this sense, investment properties are different from stocks as the majority of people don't face stocks and shares in their daily life. That is one of the reasons why real estate doesn't appear like a risky

business endeavor.

- **Hedge against inflation.** Why real estate is such a low-risk investment, and a wonderful business is that it is secured against inflation. To start with, if you choose to invest in rental properties, you can increase your rent in small amounts with a general increase in the price level. This way, you will never lose money as a landlord because of inflation. Averagely, the rise in the price of real estate is higher than inflation.

- **Part-time investment.** You can choose to leave your current job and begin a career in real estate investing. However, you can still become a part-time investor like the way many people in the industry do. Part-time is the best option for new investors as your job will present you with the financial resources to live and take care of your family until your real estate business grows.

- **Different financing options.** Since you don't need a lot of knowledge to start real estate investing, you also don't need millions of dollars to do so. Because of the multiple financing options which real estate provides to investors, you can modify your choice to the budget they have at their disposal. If you invest in a REIT, you can use as much as a few hundred dollars. If you get into a partnership, you can also get started with very little initial capital. When you purchase rental properties, you can make a 20% down payment and earn a mortgage loan for the entire price of the property. Even if you don't get approval for a mortgage, you can look for the best hard money lenders.

- **Expand your investment portfolio.** Most investors wait for an opportunity to expand their investment portfolio. Real estate properties present you with this option. You can make use of the equity of your current rental properties or the rental income from them to purchase a property. Successful real estate investors buy a new property every 2-3 years.

- **Continuous income.** Everyone invests to make money–that's the main purpose of any investment activity. But, small investments provide a source of instant and ongoing income. Once you buy a rental property, you can begin to rent it out and make money from it. As long as you can find tenants, you will gain a rental income monthly basis.

- **Long-term appreciation.** The short-term financial advantages are not the only means in which you can generate money with real estate. Natural appreciation means that the value of your property will increase with time. So, once you feel the right time has arrived to sell your property, its value will significantly be higher compared to what it was worth when you purchased it.

## Disadvantages of Real Estate

Real estate investing also comes with disadvantages to carefully factor before jumping in.

- **It requires money.** You need money to make money. Forget the gurus who promise you that you can get started in real estate with no money. Well, you will need some money to get started. You will need money to pay as a down payment plus closing costs and money to improve and update the property to optimize the rental income. And once you own the property, there will be ongoing costs such as property taxes, mortgage payments, insurance, and property maintenance.
- **Real estate requires a lot of time.** You need to set time to manage your real estate investments. There's a learning curve, and you can lose a lot of money in real estate if you don't know what to do. Besides that, actively controlling your rental properties can be time-consuming.
- **Sometimes, it can be problematic.** Tenants can result in problems and cost you time and money in court. If you own rental properties, your cash flow can take a massive hit if you end up renting to a tenant who doesn't

pay, leaves the property in poor condition when they move out, or both.

- **Rental property requires maintenance.** Rental property requires maintenance. Owners of rental property are accountable for repairs. Repairs may lead to major expenses. Replacing the HVAC or any other thing can be expensive, especially for a large property. If repairs aren't done in a "reasonable time frame" set by the local authority, you can be penalized. Insurance and taxes can also be expensive for rental property.

- **Finding finances.** Lending institutions are keen about whom they lend to, normally demanding a 20% or more down payment. Sometimes, getting a loan for investment property presents a huge problem.

- **Debt.** Investors always have the cash to pay instantly for a property. However, they go for loans. This increases the amount of debt for the investor. If you buy a property for flipping and it doesn't sell, you are stuck with the debt and with paying on the debt until the property sell.

**Real Estate Investor Mindset and Behavior**

There's a lot to say about making money in real estate investing. However, sometimes, it looks like a lot is being said about how to go about it. While it's important to learn the steps you must take to become a successful real estate investor. Most people indeed overlook the most important aspect to become successful.

Mindset: The Important Element of Generating Money in Real Estate Investing

If you want to earn money in real estate investing, you must have the right mindset. Follow these steps, and you will have the correct mindset to start generating money in real estate and repeat this year after year:

1. **Patience is a virtue.** If it were possible to get rich overnight, we'd all be

wealthy. Why most people are not is that they don't have the patience. They don't want investment to grow. They want to see it increase fast during the first week of the month. Some people begin to worry after 24 hours. You can have all the money in the world, but if you don't have the patience, nothing else matters. Remember, generating money in real estate doesn't demand the patience of a monk.

2. **Be focused on your desired result.** You must keep thinking about the goal you are after. While staying focused might make you somehow impatient at first, in the long-term, it's the best supplement. Other investment opportunities will fight for your attention. There will always be attractive elements you'll want to chase. If you can remind yourself about all that you need to gain by staying disciplined, you'll have an easier time ignoring these short-term enticements.

3. **Avoid being emotional.** It is awesome to make money in real estate. And so, you need to put your emotions aside when it comes to time to invest in real estate properties. As an investor, you should remember that expenses and excitement are their enemies. The same is true for those interested in generating money in real estate. You will not make it if you throw money at opportunities when you feel indestructible because the market is doing well and then instantly try to sell your property once it goes the other way. Being emotional at times is okay; it is human nature. However, letting those emotions control you will cost you.

4. **Set education a priority.** Making money in real estate doesn't demand extensive knowledge of physics. As you become successful, you need to look forward to even learning more because you will have firsthand experience with its advantages. It's when you get started that it can sometimes become difficult. Again, that's when patience is a big asset.

5. **Become action-oriented**. Most people would love to enjoy the advantages of investing in real estate. However, they never do because they don't take action. Taking action may mean educating yourself about real estate

investing. It may mean defining a budget, so you have the money to invest. Maybe it's finally speaking to your spouse concerning this opportunity. Whatever the cause, there comes a time when you have thought enough, and you need to do something about it.

6. **Understand what bad advice is and ignore it at all costs.** Good judgment results in success. Good judgment is normally the result of experience. Some people have no problem taking action. Maybe the problem is that you take action far too often. Even if that's not the case now, this is still an important step to creating the type of mindset relevant for making money in real estate. So if you know you're fighting indecision, this advice will finally apply. The reason is that the world is full of bad advice. As time goes by, knowing bad advice will become second nature.

7. **Learn to avoid well-intentioned detractors.** Some of your family and friends may attempt to convince you that generating money in real estate isn't the best goal for you. That's not to mean that they don't have the best of intentions. Of course, they do, but that doesn't mean they're right. Unless your friend has more experience with making money in the real estate sector than you or the person you're learning from, you should perhaps ignore their advice. You don't need to become rude. Appreciate them for their concern and tell them why you know investing makes sense for you.

In summary, real estate investing is a great way to make long-term wealth, if your head is in the perfect place, to deal with all the obstacles along the way. Success is never easy, but it is always possible with the correct real estate investing mindset. Discover your way to wealth with the help of the above tips.

## Chapter 3: Tips for Beginners

Real estate investment is the act of buying and selling houses and other property types. It is divided into two main groups: commercial and residential real estate. Residential real estate includes houses and property that will be used by individual families or persons. Commercial real estate requires buildings and properties that are supposed to be used by businesses. The real estate business is attractive and dynamic to entrepreneurs. They are attracted to it because of the amount of money required in every transaction. Unlike other trades, transactions in real estate can have values of millions. For that reason, everyone wants to get a piece of the real estate business pie.

The idea of generating money in real estate appears out of reach to some, and so, they avoid real estate investing altogether. To get you started, here are the best real estate investing tips for beginners:

**Keep reading and read more.** This list of the best tips for beginner real estate investors would be incomplete without telling the new investors to read everything they can about owning, buying, and managing an investment property. Don't be overwhelmed by all the posts, books, and guides on becoming the best real estate investor. Instead, concentrate on reading about the basics of generating money in real estate.

A good start would be to follow this book of real estate investing, and research anything that pops up that you aren't familiar with.

Don't assume you can learn everything in one day or even from reading. Successful real estate investors are still learning things every day, with the trend changing in the real estate market. Stay patient and understand that with experience, real estate investing will become second-hand nature.

**Research the prices of houses or properties in the area before investing.** This is normally the first step to do when you want to invest in some real estate. Check to find out the prices of other homes or buildings in the area and compare them with what you are being asked to pay. Also, determine the rate of acceleration of the prices in that area. Compare the price with the cost of the same type of property in other urban areas around your specific location. This will provide you with a clear picture of demand.

Additionally, you will be able to tell whether you are getting a fair price or getting ripped off. To boost your profit margin, you must buy some real estate at the lowest price that you can. Therefore, this procedure is critical.

**Learn to identify a great location.** Buying an investment property begins with selecting a better location for real estate investment. As a beginner real estate investor, this could be a little less intuitive for you. The best way to start is to find out what cities real estate experts say about thriving real estate markets. In most cases, real estate experts identify the neighborhoods that are good for real estate investing.

Don't blindly follow guides about the best places or cities for real estate investing. First, try to understand why these locations are best for purchasing an investment property. If you take the time to learn this, you will be able to know the best real estate markets on your own.

**Search for any catalysts.** Catalysts in real estate refer to developments going on around your target location that is likely to boost the value of your investment once they are active. A good example of a catalyst is the infrastructure. If you see roads, malls, and schools being built, it means that the area has a great potential for growth, and the value of your investment will rise. Not only do catalysts increase the final value of your property, but they also maintain the tax low.

**Make logical decisions, not emotional ones.** You might see a piece of real estate and start to imagine how you love it, and it would be a great choice to add to your portfolio. When you are looking for homes or other properties to invest in, don't commit because of your emotions. Make sure that you first analyze its value critically. Evaluate its numbers and watch out how it could perform for you. Purchasing some real estate because you've fallen in love with a property can cause you to buy the house at a very high price. This will make it difficult for you to generate profit afterward. Let your numerical evaluation direct you when buying a real estate.

**Understand the ins and outs of investment property analysis.** Once you have identified a location for buying an investment property, it's time to select a property. There are many factors to selecting a great income property, besides the location. For example, what type of return on investment will a single-family home income property generate? Investment property analysis will help figure out this.

However, don't try investment property analysis without using an investment property calculator. It can set a world of difference when doing investment property analysis for the first time.

**Start small.** Get started with just a single property or a duplex property that has only a few units. Don't dive in with multiple properties. As you become more experienced, you can purchase more real estate and get more active, but don't burn out early.

**Don't rush.** It can be tempting to rush into a purchase, but you need to take your time. As a new real estate investor, you should master the market conditions, like the number of properties you are renting for, how they hold their value for resale, and the neighborhood factors.

You may see a hundred properties before you decide to buy one. It is a huge decision and commitment, so take your time.

**Put aside money to cover the expected and unexpected costs involved in real estate.** Everyone understands that real estate isn't a cheap endeavor. You need to have enough capital to start with. Buying prices require huge amounts of money. Additionally, if you buy certain real estate and then rent it out, you should expect to incur some maintenance costs. The tenants are bound to destroy their houses over time. Repairing these damages before you sell the building can cost you a lot of cash. For that reason, you need to set aside some money for these repairs.

Additionally, you should always be ready for a reduction in the value of your real estate investment. Sometimes, the market drops, and as a result, you must have the finances to cover your costs in case it happens.

**Build a team to complete your vision.** When you dive into the real estate business, your rewards can be many. You can finally have a portfolio that is worth hundreds of millions of dollars. To accomplish this, you must have a committed team of agents working with you. You can only reach far if you decide to do this business on your own. Moreover, many people collaborating can share knowledge, information, and also keep each other inspired. Develop a team of highly skilled and trusted individuals before you start to invest in real estate.

**Don't overpay with real estate market analysis.** Real estate market analysis is important to pay the correct price for an investment property. The right price is the secret to getting the best profit on investment. Learn how to conduct real estate market analysis, find several real estate comparables, and determine the correct price of the income property. Not only will this ensure that you don't overpay for a single-family home, but real estate market analysis can also help find rental properties listed below market value.

Don't select only one real estate comparable. It may take a little more work to get three to five real estate comps, but it will provide you with accurate real estate market analysis results.

**Become serious with rental property management.** Poor rental property management can be the main reason why an income property fails. The work doesn't stop once you buy an investment property. Rental property management takes some time to learn, but it will be worth it when you experience high occupancy rates and a stable rental income.

Don't ignore the landlord-tenant relationship. Simple things such as listening to comments from tenants can create a healthy landlord-tenant relationship. This helps landlords in generating money in real estate.

**Consider turnkey properties.** Turnkey properties are best for beginners in real estate investing because professionals have already selected rental properties for you in great locations. They get the tenants for turnkey properties and even offer rental property management.

To succeed as a real estate investor in turnkey properties, you need to spend time to learn from the company of turnkey properties. Why did it select the location for the turnkey properties? How does it go about filling vacancies? How does it deal with rental property management for turnkey properties? Sitting back and not utilizing this real estate investment learning opportunity would be a great mistake.

Make sure that you don't jump into turnkey properties without researching the company and carrying out investment property analysis and real estate market analysis on the turnkey properties.

## Chapter 4: Question from Beginners

Whether an investor is buying their first property or their fifth home, the buying process can trigger many feelings and emotions. One of the best ways to ensure the process doesn't overwhelm you is to be well-educated and ready for the process.

There are always many questions that home buyers will have in the entire process. Even an experienced investor can forget exactly how the process works and what the proper steps are to make sure the process is relatively smooth.

When buying a house, one of the most important things to remember is that "no question is a dumb question." If you aren't sure of something when buying a property, ask!

There are many questions that beginner investors ask. Some questions are before the buying process, during a house hunt, or after an offer is accepted. Here are top frequently asked questions from beginner investors:

### Is Real Estate Investing a Way to Get Rich Quick?

The simple answer is no. While some people have made millions from the property, don't be deceived that real estate investing is a way to get rich quickly. If you want to generate a good passive income, then it would be better to consider property as one of your ways for wealth creation.

However, be aware that real estate investing is not a short term to get a rich quick channel. If done well and with guidance, you will gain:

- A huge cash flow: you will earn massive monthly passive income
- A legacy to pass down to the coming generations
- Amazing capital growth

If you are seriously considering real estate investment as a career choice, kindly note that you need to view it as more than a hobby. This means you need to dedicate some effort for it to work. If you only consider property as a hobby, you will only accomplish little profits. Your goals of generating millions from the property will remain just dreams.

Real estate investment, like any business, is a serious business, and you need to invest with the right mindset. Working only one day a week on this business is not enough, especially when you're getting started.

If you have a genuine passion for real estate, you can be successful in a shorter period, but even that will not be in the first month. There is no short cut or get rich formula in real estate. Investing has and always will be about the effort, education, and commitment you put in, regardless of what you may see on TV.

**Can I Invest in Real Estate Without Money?**

If you don't have money, then you will need to look for alternative ways to fund your real estate investment. In other words, you will need money to make money. You must come up with ways to understand, recognize, and use other people's money.

Most real estate investors think that money will make or break a deal. A lack of cash can stop a prospective buyer from bidding on a property. However, it is still possible to buy real estate with no money from the buyer's pockets. If the deal is good, the funding can easily fall into place.

Investing in real estate by borrowing money from your friends, relatives, or banking institutions is a genuine strategy for some of the best real estate investing business.

While you can invest in real estate by depending on funding from other sources, if you still can't get the funding, you will need to consider other methods to contribute resources. Keep in mind, there are many ways to support a real estate deal, and if you cannot raise money, what else can you bring?

**Can I Invest in Real Estate If I Have a Full-Time Job?**

Many people are thinking about whether it's wise to invest in real estate even with a full-time job. The second-thought is understandable. After all, many people think of a real estate investor as that person who is completely committed to the real estate industry–someone who's always moving around dressed in a suit, tie, and looking for properties.

While that image has some truth, it is only a small part of the bigger picture. There are many types of real estate investing. Sadly, many people think it's the kind that you can see on TV or with gurus where it's not so much investing as it is gambling.

The fact is that you can invest in real estate even with a full-time job. There are numerous ways to get your feet in the real estate investing sector. Some methods demand that you commit forty or more hours per week while sacrificing your social life. However, some ways will only require less than 40 hours per year, or somewhere you get to select how much time you invest. The secret is that the amount of time you commit will grow your real estate business.

While the answer to the question is yes, it comes with the warning that you won't grow your real estate business quickly as you would if you were doing it full time. However, this does not mean that you should quit your day job to concentrate on real estate investing. There are situations where it's good to play it slow and steady.

With the correct approach, the right strategies, and the right network-any new investor can succeed without quitting their job and spending 40-hours a week analyzing every deal and getting their hands on every step of the project.

If you want to move forward in your career, there's no need to sacrifice your goals to generate cash. Network with the right individuals and use systems of delegation to work for you, not against you.

**Pros of Investing While Working Full-Time**

Maintaining your full-time job has its benefits. Those working full-time in real estate investing are also held by their results. The part-time investor can live off their nine to five-placing you in a position to earn all the extra cash flow from your deals.

Also, you have an easier route to get long-term bank financing thanks to the stable income from work, which also allows you to increase and stabilize your wealth.

You can invest in real estate while maintaining your day job by doing the following:

- Invest in a buy-and-hold property with real estate investment.
- Serve as a private or hard money lender.

- Partner in a massive piece of property.

However, in the end, you need to weigh your options. If you love real estate investing and you dislike your full-time job, there's no point in being undecided. Just ensure that you set up a small nest before you get all your feet into full-time real estate investing.

**Do I Need a Real Estate License?**

It depends on what kind of real estate investing you are going for. If you're going to buy an investment property, below are some real estate investment types that you can do without getting a license:

1. **Real estate wholesaling.** Wholesaling is one of the best investment strategies for beginners that have some knowledge in sales. The whole idea behind wholesaling is getting an investment property from a seller, then looking for a property buyer and assigning the contract to the buyer at a higher price. Wholesalers purchase contracts for low prices and also sell them low at a profit. This works a lot like flipping properties, except there's no maintenance required in the process.

2. **Airbnb investment properties.** Airbnb investment properties have become popular because of the popularity of Airbnb. Airbnb investment properties are short term rental vacation that generates a lot of income than traditional investment properties, but they're also affected by the seasons and tourism sector. Airbnb rentals are considered the newest real estate investment strategies that investors invest more and more in it as time passes. Airbnb investment properties are a great opportunity because they present the stability of a rental property while utilizing the space maximum capacity.

3. **The infamous buy and hold.** The buy and hold strategy is as old as the

real estate investment business itself. The real estate investor buys a given property and rents it out for rental income. The main attraction of this method is that the real estate investor can purchase investment properties through financing and then leasing the properties to tenants, which generates a monthly rental income that covers the mortgage payments.

In summary, remember that if you're looking into becoming a real estate agent, it's a completely different story. You'll have to go through a process to get licensed and start working.

**Do I Need an LLC or Corporation to Invest in Real Estate?**

No. It's not a must to have an LLC. However, real estate investment creates inherent liabilities. Whether you invest in apartments or homes, areas such as staircases or rooms, all have a high risk of exposure. Even tenants carry the risk of exposing you to liability from potential environmental–contamination, slip-and-fall claims, and other injury claims. This is why steps should be taken to safeguard yourself, such as creating a Limited Liability Company.

An LLC is a great way of protecting your assets. It is known for combining the best features of a corporation and a partnership. An LLC allows you to protect your assets from claims by creditors against the LLC. In other words, you attain personal liability protection.

While an LLC is the popular option and usually the best one, you need to familiarize yourself with the different corporate structures and whether a corporation may suit more with the goals you have for your portfolio or the business performed by the organization.

**How Can I Learn from Other Investors?**

Fortunately, there are plenty of ways you can learn from other investors. Successful investors have created both free and premium resources that you can get and learn from them.

Like any other activity, you need to begin by learning the theory first. Here are the best ways you can learn from other investors:

**Official real estate education.** You can go for an official real estate education, this one will not only concentrate on how to invest in real estate, but you'll learn more. You'll learn theory, research techniques, and different types of investment strategies.

But, not every career path requires an official education. For example, if you want to be a real estate developer, you need this kind of education, or else you don't stand a chance to succeed. However, when you consider renting a home and have no idea how to do it right, there's no need for a few years of education in a college.

**Real estate investment books.** Real estate investment books written by successful investors are another great source of information a beginner investor can use. Whenever you have a specific question, for example, concerning real estate market analysis, you can get the answer in books.

Additionally, once you're ready to learn more about purchasing an investment property, for instance, you can use this information on the topic you need at any given moment. This is a good thing for people who have a full-time job and can't fit courses into their schedule. Besides, you can use books as referrals along the way if you want.

The best thing about real estate investment books is that they're written by professors and successful individuals. Additionally, you can typically trust the information given there. You should also learn more about the author to make sure you're receiving sound advice.

**Real estate websites.** Real estate blogs and websites can be great sources. Any small question related to buying an investment property, running investment analysis, etc. can be located within seconds as you search the web for a given topic. The best thing is that the information is more relevant and up to date than books or even some courses that follow an outdated curriculum. But, don't be quick to trust all real estate websites. Choose only the professional ones.

**Podcasts.** There is a lot of excellent real estate investing podcasts available for free. Although the format is similar to blogs than books, a 1-hour podcast episode can go further than your average blog article. Podcasts can also expose you to a wide variety of perspectives in your real estate education,

**Seminars.** Do you want to learn real estate investing face-to-face? You can attend in-person conferences and seminars. However, remember that the truly educational ones are not free. A complete weekend seminar could put you back a few thousand dollars.

Before you sign up for an in-person seminar, ensure you do your homework and read reviews on the event and the presenters. The best seminars can be a great way to network and learn real estate investing; they can still cost you if you don't do your research.

**How Can I Pay Less Taxes to Start?**

**Hold properties for more than a year**. When you own something for less than a year and sell it for a profit, that profit is deducted at your normal income tax rate. That applies to flip properties and anything that involves purchasing low and selling high.

If you flip more than one or two properties in a year, you run the risk of the IRS categorizing you as a self-employed "dealer" and subjecting your earnings to double FICA taxes.

One way to avoid this is to own properties for longer than a year before selling. This eliminates the risk of being categorized as a dealer and diverts your profits from being taxed as normal income to being taxed as capital gains. For many Americans, capital gains are deducted at 15%–significantly less than most American's normal income tax rates.

If you flip properties, choose to rent them for a one-year lease term before selling them. You reduce your tax rate, earn some cash flow, and could even gain from appreciation and a higher sales price.

**Don't pay double FICA taxes.** FICA taxes refer to employment taxes meant to fund Social Security and Medicare. They're divided between employers and employees, with every party paying 7.65%. If you're self-employed, you owe both, for a total sum of 15.3% plus your federal, state, and local income taxes.

Any individual who flips properties should create a means to avoid a dealer classification by the IRS and thus avoid this extra 15.3% tax. One way you can avoid the dealer's status is to define "investment intent" for the profits of each sale. This means, develop a case that you don't sell properties as part of your regular business practice, but to produce capital for other investment projects.

Another way is to avoid doing business through a single-member LLC, which is normally disregarded for tax purposes. However, you can generate an entity such as a partnership LLC or S-corp that changes how investors are deducted.

Speak to an accountant with a lot of experience working with real estate investors if you want to flip more than a couple of properties every year. Like many other parts of the tax code, this one contains gray areas, so you need to set a persuasive case for a non-dealer status if the IRS challenges you.

**Live in the house for two years.** Have you ever considered a live-in flip? You move in, and over time, make changes. If you live in the property for at least two years, the first $250,000 capital gains are tax-free for singles. For married people, the limit is a full $500,000.

Of course, you might not want to live in a constant work zone or move every two years, but if you love property improvement and tinkering around the house, it can be a great way to earn money tax-free.

**Optimize your deductions.** One of the benefits of real estate investing is that every real estate cost, and some paper costs, are tax-deductible. You can remove:

- Property taxes
- Insurance
- Advertising expenses
- Legal fees
- Home office expenses
- Mortgage interest
- Depreciation

The best thing is that you can still take the normal deduction. Most of these don't demand you to categorize your deductions; they deduct the amount of total taxable income on your schedule.

**Achieve appreciation by borrowing, not selling.** The property you purchased above for $150, 000 appreciates over time. After some years, you will have built some equity in it.

You can sell it and pay capital gains taxes on that equity, or you can borrow against the property and not pay any taxes on your cash in hand. You'll have to reduce the borrowing costs, both closing costs and mortgage interest.

As time goes, your tenants pay the loan off for you. You have to maintain the property, which continues to appreciate for you, and the rents increase with time, even as your mortgage payment remains fixed. And when the loan is paid off, you can turn around and borrow more cash against your property.

**Go for an installment sale.** For example, you sell a property for a $50,000 profit. For whatever reason, you don't want to perform a 1031 exchange to purchase a new property right away. If you file your tax return with an additional $50,000 in taxable income in one year, you can expect to pay some hefty taxes on it, which might as well push you into a huge tax bracket.

Also, you can spread the profit over many years by providing seller financing. In the year that you sell the property, you only have to pay income taxes on whatever down payment and principal the buyer pays you. With time, they gradually pay down the balance they owe you, month by month, and year by year. To make things better, you get to charge the buyer's interest.

Of course, the risk is that the default, and you have to foreclose on the property. Don't get into an installment sale lightly and ensure that you qualify the buyer. One way is to start with a lease-purchase agreement, where the buyer begins as a renter with part of their rent going towards their down payment every month.

**Own properties in a self-directed IRA.** You're perhaps familiar with IRAs and Roth IRAs as a tax-deferred means to invest for retirement. What you might not be aware of is that you can set up your normal own self-directed IRA and use it to invest in real estate tax-free.

Be careful. This isn't as simple as purchasing equities in a normal IRA. First, you need to get a custodian company to administer the self-directed IRA for you. They build the self-directed IRA, and you transfer money into it. Next, you can create a legal entity, such as an LLC, to buy and own investment properties. The self-directed IRA invests money into the legal entity as your selected investment.

Where things become, the complex is if you want to finance the investment property instead of buying it in cash. Financing is supported, but it comes with some vital caveats. The loan must be "non-recourse," meaning the borrower can't be individually liable, which most lenders don't support. Also, only the normal IRA rules apply. You cannot withdraw money before the age of 59.5, and you must begin withdrawing by the age of 70.5.

If you want to invest in real estate using a self-directed IRA, begin by researching custodians and speaking with them about the process and their fees.

**Die owning your properties.** If you die owning real estate, the acquisition cost disappears, and your heirs pay no capital gains, or you can earn the rent from the property every month, and never sell it. If you want to pull out cash, you can borrow against it, or you could leave it unencumbered and generate more cash flow from it.

**Final Thought**

If you want to win at the game of wealth, you must know the rules. And no place is clearer than learning how to reduce your income taxes.

Learn how to optimize the tax advantages provided to real estate owners. For the rest of your life, they can save you hundreds of thousands of dollars or more and allow you to put more of your money toward creating wealth.

## Chapter 5: Which Properties to Choose

Real estate investing is much more than purchasing a property, and expecting its value will increase. You also need to know the types of real estate investment properties and how they can generate the biggest profit on your investment.

If you want to make it as a real estate investor, you're going to need to purchase a property at some point. And, the type of property you purchase could predict your future as a real estate investor. Remember, there are many different investment strategies present in real estate investing.

Well, why are property types so vital in real estate investing? The answer is that each property generates profits in different ways. To get started, here is a description of the main types of real estate investment properties.

### Residential Real Estate Investing

Residential properties consist of single-family homes, townhomes, mobile homes, and condos. Each type can generate investment profit in various ways.

For instance, you can purchase a single-family home and hold it until its value increases, or you can rent it out while you wait for the value to increase.

You can invest in multi-unit properties to generate income from different sources. For instance, some skilled investors got their start by purchasing a four-unit property while living in a single unit and renting it out the other three units.

Mobile homes, condos, townhomes all provide multiple investment strategies. You can invest in a mobile home park and get income from different rental units, or you can purchase a condo or townhouse and wait for the value to increase.

Most successful investors purchase more than one townhouse or condo in the same complex. This method allows them to control their properties more efficiently because there are in the same location.

**Single-Family Homes**

If you're getting started in real estate investment, it's better to go for a single-family home. There are pros and cons to either choice, but overall, single-family homes are the best investment. Here are a couple of things to consider:

- **Higher rent income.** With single-family homes, you can rent a property for much more money than an apartment. The flip side is that apartment buildings generate multiple rent checks. However, these checks come with extra responsibilities and duties.
- **Utility bills.** When you let a single-family property, the tenants are always accountable for all the utility payments. In an apartment building, the landlord always pays the water, sometimes even gas and electricity. You will not be subject to waste and abuse if the tenants are footing the bill.
- **Faster appreciation.** Location is significant, and there are many factors to consider, but single family homes cost less and appreciate faster than multiple-family units. It's all numbers on paper until you sell the property, but it's great to see your investment grow when your appraised value increases. The investment isn't risky because you're spending less money than on an apartment building. Your mortgage will be manageable and can be handled by your tenant's monthly payments.
- **Great tenants.** At every income level, you'll meet good and bad people, but house renters are more responsible than apartment dwellers. They take care of their yards and are likely to pay their rent on time. People who rent

a house are likely to stay longer. You won't have to deal with space, turnover, or interviewing prospective renters. People who rent your house will take care of it as if it's their home. They will treat it better, especially if they want to buy it in the future.

- **Less maintenance.** Single-family homes have only a single furnace, one laundry machine, and probably two toilets. Multiple-family dwellings have different appliances and fixtures which will demand your attention. This can be frustrating, expensive, and time-consuming. Tenants living in a single-family home may take care of these things themselves, and you'll have fewer things to worry about.

- **You can do it yourself.** You can easily control a single property on your own. If you rent an apartment building, you will have many tenants and demand extra maintenance. You would employ a property manager to deal with all the duties and unwanted surprises that come with renting multiple units. With a single house, you'll have frequent repairs and be required to handle them, but you can do it yourself. If you are handy, you can make small repairs. If not, you can create a relationship with professionals in your place so you can call on them when there is an issue. You will not require a property manager or partner. You decide yourself, and you won't have to divide your earnings.

Of course, there's no guarantee in the real estate market. You can either have a poor experience running a single-family home or a better experience running an apartment complex. But keep these points in mind when planning to invest in real estate. You can venture into multiple units to expand your portfolio but begin with a single-family home to gain experience and see whether it's right for you.

**Commercial Properties**

At its core, commercial real estate refers to any property used for retail reasons or office space. Investors purchase these properties and rent them to business owners who require space to run their companies or buy and sell goods and services.

The commercial properties you're perhaps most familiar with include retail stores, restaurants, or the place where you go to work.

Unfortunately, investing in commercial real estate is a bit complex and expensive than residential real estate. For starters, the information to verify is whether a commercial property is a great investment.

Also, renting a commercial property isn't as easy as drawing up a real contract. You may require a detailed lease agreement.

If you plan to finance your commercial properties, you can expect to pay a minimum down payment of 25-50%. You'll require good credit, and in some situations, banks may need you to have a lease in place from a company that's already renting a space in the property.

Lastly, figuring out the value of your property isn't as simple as comparing other commercial properties around your location. The type of business and the amount it generates in sales impacts the value of your building.

**Facts About Becoming a Commercial Real Estate Investor**

Becoming a commercial real estate investor requires that you invest in any non-residential real estate that is used for business reasons only. Commercial real estate consists of office buildings, warehouses, retail properties, and shopping centers. As with most investments, investing in commercial property has risks and rewards. However, becoming a commercial real estate investor can be a great way to diversify your investment portfolio.

Before you get started, newbie investors should have a great knowledge of this investment method so that they can make an informed decision. There are some features of commercial real estate investing that you need to factor before you go down this path.

**Demands large initial investment.** Becoming a commercial real estate investor can be an expensive venture than becoming a real estate residential investor because of the large initial capital requirement. It might require large loans. Thus, it's important to have enough capital upfront when purchasing commercial real estate than buying residential real estate in the same location. Even so, receiving funds from banks can be easier for a great commercial real estate property.

Also, once you find the best commercial real estate, you can expect large capital expenditures to happen. Because there are more facilities to maintain, the expenses will be more. This makes investing in shopping centers and office buildings the best endeavor for most investors.

Many real estate investors fail to get into the market because of this. So the benefit to the huge financial requirements is that there is low competition.

**Has a higher profit.** Overall, becoming a commercial real estate investor has many risks; it guarantees a higher profit than residential property investing. The outcome on commercial property is higher, both on investment and per square foot basis. This is true if you choose to rent or lease a multi-unit commercial property. More space results in more tenants, which leads to more income generated. While the average profit on an investment of commercial real estate varies from 6-12%, that of residential properties is normally between 1-4%. But the profit on investment will also vary based on the type of property, vacancy rate, costs of property management, and other factors.

Commercial real estate leases are also longer than residential leases. Most commercial leases are at least three years. This enables a commercial real estate investor to predict annual cash flow, have lower vacancy rates, and lower turnover costs. The disadvantage to longer lease terms is that it is difficult for a commercial real estate investor to break a long-term lease if they feel unhappy with a tenant.

**Has more risks.** Whether you're investing in commercial or residential property, it's important to keep your risks low. But, becoming a commercial real estate investor is riskier than investing in residential property. Besides the fact that it demands a larger cash outlay, you'll be putting all your eggs in one basket if a single commercial property is all you can manage.

Spending all your funds into a single commercial property is riskier than spreading the risk across different residential properties. If you miss your mark with a single-family home, it will not be a huge financial obstacle as skipping your mark with commercial property. It is easy to diversify and spread out your risk across different residential properties that are in various locations.

Also, the risks of real estate investing for a commercial real estate investor will change depending on the investment property type. The risks related to two commercial buildings in the same place would change independently. On the other hand, residential properties that are close to each other would reveal the risk. It is critical to understand the level of risk connected with your prospective investment.

**Susceptible to economic volatility.** The property market is unpredictable and always changing. However, commercial real estate is more vulnerable to economic slumps than residential real estate. Therefore, commercial real estate investing becomes even riskier.

In case of an economic drop, people might close their businesses, look for other jobs, or even work from home. Residential properties will always have a relatively high demand even when the housing market is worse. People will always want a place to live no matter the economic situation. Residential properties perform more consistently than commercial real estate during the economic crisis.

But it's difficult for a commercial real estate investor to get a commercial loan in a worse economy. This makes buying or selling commercial property more difficult.

**Raw land.** The advantages of investing in raw land can be significant, but only if you play your game right. Land refers to undeveloped land without property built on it. If you are not building, banks will consider it as a "speculative investment" and might not approve your home loan. Learn how to qualify.

**Inland Properties**

Compared to other investments, land doesn't need much involvement. It can be a passive long-term investment for you.

Even more, you could manage to purchase smaller pieces of land with money alone. Insurance, property taxes, or maintenance aren't too high.

Competition is a bit low so that you can get a great deal more easily. People with a smaller budget can buy now and build later. This ensures that they can't be priced out of the property market later on.

While its value may increase slowly, land prices can increase overnight. Some people purchase land, thinking the government will rezone it soon. Once rezoned, the value of land increases, and they can sell it to a developer. You can also select what you want to do with the land. Based on the situation, you can sell it to a developer or build it yourself.

Despite that, investing in raw land can be difficult. Invest only if you know what you're doing.

**Office Properties**

Office buildings can generate high returns, and long-term leases mean less management. The drawback, nothing seems to increase as much as office rents and office occupancy rates.

There are risks with office properties. The biggest one is that the rental rates can increase and decrease with the economy. In the worst moments, the same number of individuals require housing, but there can be a significant drop in the number of businesses or at least the number that is searching for an office to rent.

Office buildings vary from large multi-tenant buildings in city business districts to single-tenant buildings. Rents and valuations are affected by employment growth, a region's economic concentration, and productivity rates. Individualized tenant improvements are generally not very involved, but the quality of tenants is significant.

Investment-grade office properties are categorized into three tiers that are determined by the location, condition of the building, and amenities. Class A buildings are the best quality, with state-of-the-art amenities and facilities, as well as having great accessibility. Class A offices generate rents that are above the market value with tenants that are premier office users. Class B offices are meant to have enough amenities, with the state of the building being good. Class B offices have average tenants who pay, on average, the market rate for space. Class C buildings comprise of anything less than Class B, with tenants who use the building for its functionality and pay below market value for space.

**Vacation Rentals**

As a busy professional, you may not have enough time to work actively as an investor. Whether it's researching the real estate market or the stock market, there is a substantial time commitment. Even the time to get in touch with financial advisors, and go through their offerings to decide whether they're right for you is heavy.

Investing in vacation rental properties is a great way to make money in real estate.

There are different benefits to buying a vacation rental property, especially for a beginner investor. **Here are some of the top benefits:**

1. **Dual-use property.** The idea of having a dual-purpose property is great, whether you're a novice real estate investor or an experienced one. With a vacation rental property, you can use the investment property to spend your holiday while renting it out part of it for the rest of the year.
2. **Easy to get tenants.** There are specific websites developed to serve guests and tenants who want vacation rental properties. In other words, you will easily find guests.

3. **Extra rental income.** A major advantage of investing in vacation rentals is that you can generate more rental income as a beginner real estate investor. If you pick a good location, vacation homes can attract many tourists and travelers in high season.

4. **Real estate appreciation.** Another benefit of owning a vacation rental is the money you can generate in the long term if you decide to sell the investment property. Vacation rentals are usually in demand; this means their values keep increasing. When the time is ready for you to sell the investment property, you make more profit because of the appreciation factor in real estate investment.

**Large Multi-family Properties**

These properties resemble townhome complexes and apartments. They are a good investment option for a person who can manage a busy schedule or a person who can hire a property management company. There are many ways to make money from large multifamily properties and can set you on the road to financial freedom.

The profit you get from these properties can be large. Most newbie investors start their career by investing in single-family homes but later upgrade to the multifamily sector. These properties are good for real estate, investing for many reasons. For example, there is a high demand for large multi-family properties. However, before you start to hunt for multi-family properties, make sure you know the cities in the US market suitable for these properties.

Several factors make a given market suitable for multifamily real estate investing. Some of these factors include a strong economy, high rental demand, and job growth. Another element to consider is the cap rate of properties in the housing market.

## Cap Rate in Real Estate Investing

Investors share the desire to get profitable properties that offer them a high return on investment. The ROI can be measured with different elements, one of which is the cap rate. This metric is the first to pop up when analyzing investment properties. It determines the rate of profit, depending on the value of the property, rental expense, and income.

Cap rate is a vital measure to determine the profitability of a given rental property or city. The three major uses of cap rate in real estate investing:

1. Return on investment
2. Screening tool
3. Level of risk

Purchasing a multi-family property can be your first step to generate wealth if you have enough capital.

If you believe that real estate is where your lack lies, you can take advantage of your first equity to make a down payment. If you know how to manage people and money, you will succeed in growing your investments.

## Chapter 6: Rental Properties Vs. Flipping Houses

If you are a beginner investor, and you want to generate money in real estate investing, the first thing you need to consider is the investment strategy to follow. The choices available are many. However, two ways are the most popular among real estate investors-rental properties and flipping houses. This takes us to the main question of this chapter: which investment method is better in real estate investing, fix-and-flip, or buying an investment property to rent?

The answer depends. You have to consider your personal goals, level of knowledge, financial position, and experience in the real estate market, etc. However, assuming you are a beginner real estate investor, and you want to take your first step in the business, most professionals will advise purchasing an investment property to rent over a fixer-upper.

In this chapter, you will learn the pros and cons of each investment strategy and discover which investment strategy is suitable for your financial goals.

Every investor has their say about which channel will generate you the most money. In theory, they can provide huge returns.

### Advantages of Flipping Houses

**Quick returns on investment.** The clearest advantage of flipping properties is immediate gratification. Instead of waiting for years to pay off the property and gain all the profits from your monthly rent check, you can enjoy instant gains when flipping a property.

Your capital is associated with a shorter period than buy-and-hold properties. As earlier said, the average timeframe on a house flip is about six months. Remember that this is an average. If this is your first experience flipping a property, expect to face a few obstacles in the road, which might very well extend your time. The faster you can flip a property, the higher the potential to earn a greater return on investment.

**No-long term property management.** You don't need to be worried about searching for tenants, collecting rent checks, and maintain the property. Flipping property allows you to evade the challenges of being a landlord.

**Work part-time.** Flipping properties doesn't demand full-time attention so you can maintain your day job and flop properties part-time to generate extra cash on the side.

Working part-time will allow you to 'get your feet wet' to find out whether flipping properties is for you before you quit your full-time gig.

**Work from your home.** When you're first getting started, you will generally be the only employee, so you don't want to rent out an expensive storefront or warehouse to control your business. You can control your whole flipping business from the comfort of your home.

**Minimal startup costs.** Many small businesses demand large startup costs for buying franchise licenses, establishing a storefront, buying large amounts of inventory or equipment.

Flipping homes requires a small amount of startup capital. If you have little-to-no money, there are creative strategies for using other people's money that you can apply to finance your first property purchase.

**No licenses or degrees.** You don't need to have a license or degree to flip houses, but it requires a specific mindset, spirit, and a specific set of skills. It's an advantage to have real estate and construction experience, but what's important is your ability to delegate tasks and concentrate on the areas of your business that you're good at and enjoy.

**Personal growth.** Flipping properties is not a straightforward process, and there will be failures, mistakes, and hardships throughout this period, but this process grants a huge opportunity for you to learn, experience, and grow on a personal level.

Starting a house business will help you learn the basics of owning and controlling your own business. As the business owner, you'll be in charge of controlling and understanding all features of the business, which can allow you to develop critical business management experience and skills.

By managing the rehab of your flip project, you will gain valuable experience and insight into all features of the construction process. You will master the processes and methods of construction and discover the costs of labor and materials, which will allow you to generate a lot of cash on future projects.

**Challenges of Flipping Property**

**Varied income.** This is where you need to analyze the opportunity cost of flipping properties. If your full-time job is flipping properties, you're giving up steady, consistent income from working in a different career.
Of course, you can generate money flipping; however, it will be significant to determine whether the money you make through flipping will generate more or less income than your current day-job.

**Taxes.** Flipping comes with the additional cost from purchasing and selling, including taxes on capital gains. Closing costs when both buying and selling a property can add up and reduce your total return on investment. Those who are self-employed pay the highest income taxes, more than 43%. Without getting into too much detail, you should expect to pay an extra 15% on top of your normal taxes.

There is a significant difference between short-term and long-term capital gains tax rates. If you own a property for less than a year, you should expect to pay a capital gains tax rate depending on your earned income.

**Potential to lose money.** One of the biggest problems in flipping properties is the risk of losing money. If you fail to resell your purchase agreement, you may end up losing your deposit when you back out, or get stuck purchasing a house that you were not planning to. Flippers who purchase properties, rehab, and sell can lose money if the costs of rehab are more than estimated.

**Ineligible for 1031 exchange.** One of the best parts of real estate ownership is the potential to do a tax-deferred exchange when you sell. The 1031 exchange enables you to avoid paying capital gains tax as long as you sell and buy more property. But you can only file 1031 only with an investment property, and flipped transactions don't qualify because they are speculative and short term.

**Rental Properties**

**Source of passive income.** The first reason why you should invest in rental properties is that they are a great source of passive income, while fixer-uppers aren't. What this means is that once your investment property is rented out, you'll have a constant stream of cash flow that comes in the form of the monthly rent. Property investors gain from this cash flow because it pays off their monthly rental expenses without having to work for it. Besides, when done right, investing in a rental property generates positive cash flow, which is crucial for any real estate investor.

On the flip side, flipped properties are cheap houses that require major improvements to sell them and make a quick return. Therefore, once you buy an investment property, it will not make any money as long as you're working on renovating it. Rental properties receive profits only after selling the fixed property. For that reason, buying an investment property to rent will require you to work as much as fix-and-flips to earn money in real estate investing.

**It has long term benefits.** With rental properties, not only will you gain from instant cash flow and rental income, but also possible real estate appreciation. By that, it means that the longer a real estate investor retains his/her investment property, the more value it will gain. Also, you gain more equity in the property if you applied for a mortgage. Long term, this will allow you to sell rental properties for a higher price than the initial buying price, generating a nice profit.

**Investment property has fewer risks.** As said before, fix-and-flips are risky real estate investments for many reasons. First, there is the risk of losing money because of not selling investment property quickly. Another reason that makes flipping properties risky is unexpected costs that could skyrocket. This includes everything from creating permit costs, material delays, contractor delays, and costs of renovations and materials you had not budgeted for. These costs will quickly increase and eat into any possible profit for property investors. You will not have to handle any of that from buying a rental property to rent.

When you buy a rental property, you can remove a lot of extra costs, such as depreciation, which will save you thousands each year in taxes.

**The rental property protects you from inflation.** Inflation occurs because of the rise in the cost of living. Overall real estate has been found to protect investors from this. This is correct for rental property investors; historically, cash flow has kept pace with inflation. In other words, as inflation happens, rental rates increase. So, if you're buying an investment property to rent and the cost of living is increasing, you, as a real estate investor, can charge your tenants higher rents, which may result in higher rental income, and if you're spending well, positive cash flow.

Also, inflation doesn't affect mortgage payments; this means they technically decrease as inflation increases. Fix-and-flips, however, are not as directly connected to inflation as rental properties because they don't generate any rental income.

While both rental properties and flipping houses are great investment techniques to generate money in real estate, experienced investors believe that purchasing an investment property to rent is a better choice than to fix-and-flip. Rental properties are passive income investments, have fewer risks, long term benefits, and protect you from inflation.

That said, let's learn how you can make any real estate property a positive cash flow investment property.

Owning a positive cash flow investment property is the main goal of every real estate investor. Once you purchase an investment property, there are two options: the real estate investor is either losing or making money. After all, this is a business where risk is a common thing. Typically, time will indicate whether you're going to be a successful real estate investor or not.

**What Does a Positive Cash Flow Investment Property Mean?**

What is meant by a positive cash flow investment property? In general, these are investment properties that are generating money. Well, any rental property generates some revenue when it's being occupied. However, for the income property to be grouped as a positive cash flow investment property, it should generate enough rental income to handle rental expenses and have money left as profit. Are you wondering how to convert your investment property into a positive cash flow investment? Keep reading.

**Rental income.** Determine the optimal rent that will be sufficient to cover rental costs. Establishing the rent isn't the hardest part if you know how to do it. You can use an online investment property calculator. This tool can help you run real estate market analysis and determine the market value of your property.

The rent is normally 0.8% to 1.1% of that value. Besides using the investment property calculator, make sure you compute the expected costs of the property while determining the rent.

Remember that if you charge too little, your rental income will not be sufficient to cover rental costs. Additionally, if you charge too high, you will not have enough demand to control an occupied property. For that reason, the real estate investor will be losing money. In both instances, if you do it wrong, your investment property will not generate positive cash flow.

**Upkeep costs and additional expenses.** You need to understand that you can't expect your investment property to generate positive cash flow if you have large rental expenses that rental income cannot cover. However, this is normal because every beginner investor wants his or her investment property to look beautiful. Therefore, investing a lot in furnishing, decoration, etc. is what most people do first. What you need to know is that most tenants prefer beautifying their home themselves, because it creates a homelike feeling. Therefore, to convert your long term rental property into a positive cash flow investment, consider deducting rental costs.

**Location.** To convert any property into a positive cash flow investment property, you need to adapt your property to the external elements, such as location. In other words, when the investment property is located in the top tourist destination, do not bother to create long-term rentals. The opportunity you will be generating cash in real estate is small. The optimal rental strategy depends on the location of your investment property.

**Choosing the optimal rental strategy.** Generating cash in real estate is the best part of this business. But, if the beginner real estate investor selects the wrong rental strategy for one of his/her income properties, making money in real estate may remain a dream. It's commonly considered that the decision of a rental strategy for the investment property depends on the investor's choice. However, this decision-making process may not always be the best thing to do.

# Chapter 7: Network of Person for Your Business

Is it time to create a real estate team? Building a team is a must.

Consider this: your clients expect it. To be a top agent today, your clients need to understand that you have the power, reach, and resources behind you. You require a buyer's agent, perhaps two or three.

This power will always be considered as valuable. It will allow you to be seen as the "THE" listing agent. Also, this business model will allow you to concentrate on listings as your major source of business; then you can point buyer clients to your buyer's agent(s), and maintain the ones you want to serve.

As a new investor, you will need virtually as many people to buy a property. Buying a home is a big investment with many variables. It is a challenge course that you will find hard to navigate on your own. You need the experience of professionals who safeguard your interests as they take you through the process of discovering a home, presenting an offer, winning financing, and completing the sale. This chapter introduces you to the real estate experts who will make up your real estate team. For each of the key players, you will get tips on how to identify the right one.

## Real Estate Agent

A real estate agent is an important member of your real estate investing team. A great real estate agent will help you get deals, bid on your behalf, master the real estate marketplace, and transact. Real estate agents can serve as a buyer or seller. Traditionally, real estate agents received a commission of about 6% by the seller of a property. As such, if you want to include a real estate agent into your team to help you purchase property, it will be free for you. Remember not to work with any real estate agent. Try to get one who is investor savvy, or has worked with other real estate investors in the past. Your real estate agent will access the Multiple Listing Service (MLS). MLS will allow you to access the latest property details when assessing the local market. Also, ensure that you select a responsive, well connected, honest, and amicable individual. Get referrals from other real estate investors, local forums, and real estate meetups.

**Getting the Best Real Estate Professional**

When selecting an agent, you want an individual who works in the business full time and has extensive knowledge of his or her field. You want a creative, hardworking, and aggressive agent, and who knows how and where to get deals.

Most real estate experts haven't worked with investors. They have never performed a creative transaction. This can be a problem for you, and it can take some time to identify the right agent, but the time you spent will be important. Since your agent is one of the most important people, he or she cannot be the weakest link in your power team chain.

One of the most critical things to consider is an agent who thinks as you do. However, most agents are not receptive to "unusual" offers. They may not believe in "nothing down" offers or creative techniques. If you plan to submit a creative offer, and you are working with an agent who doesn't think outside the box, it is time to look for a new one. At the moment, you should stress on being the one to submit the offer because you want the owner to understand the benefits of your offer. Believing in those benefits will be important in generating a convincing presentation.

Notify the agent what you are searching for and be specific. If you are going to start with the wholesale deals, let the agent know you want distressed properties that need improvement. Don't allow the agent to pre-qualify you. Let them know that you use private funding and can close quickly.

**Lenders:** Building good relationships with private money lenders and conventional lenders is important for any real estate investor. Lenders can vary from small community banks or credit unions to big national banks. Mortgage companies and brokers are also better choices. Other options for financing can be through hard money lenders. No matter which route you decide to take if or when you finance your real estate investments, the most crucial is establishing relationships with different lenders. Start building relationships with these lenders today, so when a great chance pops up, you will be ready with the right financing.

**Significant other:** Your spouse plays a big role in your real estate, investing success. Working from the same page with the person you spend the most time with can be a great success. Why you need to be on the same page with your significant other is because this person has a great impact on your free time, thoughts, money, decision-making, and ambitions.

**Contractor handyman:** Including contractors and handymen to handle the repairs is important for any real estate investor. To find these people, you can request for referrals from other real estate investors, search on craigslist.org or AngiesList.com.

Ensure you confirm their references. Request your contractor's references if they arrived on time and finished the task they said they would. Determine whether they did a great job? Are they trustworthy? Remember that the most affordable option may not be the best option. It may require some analysis to get the perfect contractor, so remain patient. Don't forget that you're building your first-class team.

**Accountant:** Getting an accountant on board is a smart choice. A certified accountant can help organize your personal and business tax profits and can provide you with important recommendations. Try to search for an accountant who has worked with other real estate experts or who is real estate savvy. Get this team member as soon as possible, because a great CPA can help you select the best tax-saving strategy for real estate investing.

**Lawyer:** An attorney is important in any real estate team. A great real estate attorney can help execute legally binding leases and other real estate documents. Try to appoint a lawyer that understands real estate or has experience working in real estate. A real estate attorney can help you decide and set up the right legal entity for holding your real estate properties.

**Property manager:** An experienced property manager is a valuable asset to your real estate investing network. From analyzing tenants to controlling property related issues, a property manager can save you from the most time-consuming tasks. Perform an intensive search to find a great property manager. Don't forget to check the references.

**Bookkeeper:** You might want to employ a bookkeeper to help maintain an accurate record of incoming credits and outgoing debits. A bookkeeper can help you monitor income and costs, and help prepare your finances for tax season. A correct account of costs and income is vital, and as you begin generating more wealth and have more properties to account for, a great bookkeeper can be useful.

**Insurance agent:** You might think all insurance brokers are the same, but they aren't. Some insure investment property, and some don't. Some approve properties you're going to flip, and some don't. You want to get a local who can help you with your insurance needs.

**Birddog:** These are individuals who may have a full-time job but have the kind of jobs where they're always out and about and may have the upper hand for possible opportunities. These are also individuals who want to become real estate investors and want to share leads with other investors for a given fee.

**Well-connected business experts:** You might be wondering what is a well-connected business expert? These are people who work closely in your niche. They know everyone in the area and how to make things happen.

These are important people to have on your real estate team to establish a long-term relationship. These are people you want to find the means to help. Keep in mind that the relationship is a two-way street.

**Cleaning company:** You may not need this company for a while, but when you are almost ready to list your rental after rehab, you will need this company then. Again, it will be wonderful for you to find a company that you can offer repeat business as you expand your portfolio.

**Tips to Start Building a Successful Real Estate Team**

**Define goals.** The first thing is to set your goals and expectations.
This will allow you to set up your general objectives and a purpose for your new team. Also, building clear goals will allow you to develop a simple structure for paying your new team members.

Lay down things that your business has to gain by adding more team members, and what you expect to achieve through hiring.

Remember to define SMART goals. In other words, the goals should be Specific, Measurable, Achievable, Relevant, and Time-bound.

**Determine who to employ.** Once you set your goals, the next step is to decide on the real estate team duties you'll want to fill. Most importantly:

- How many people do you want to fulfill your goals?
- Who should you employ first?

**Get a personal assistant.** The first individual to hire when developing a real estate team should be an admin. This individual can take the administrative roles off your plate so you can concentrate on selling and client relations.

This individual can work from home, remotely, or as a virtual assistant. Some of the things they can do include:

- Respond to phone calls and emails
- Prepare documents
- Update listings
- Schedule booking meetings
- Order supplies

As you can see, the role of an assistant is big for creating your real estate team. Consider the time you can free up for drinking coffee with clients or display properties when these tasks are off your plate.

**Define your real estate team compensation strategy.** Once you have established who to employ, know how much of your budget will be allocated to these employees. To figure this out, you need to consider two real estate team models. These comprise of the employee model and the independent contractor model.

- **Employees.** If you want your new hires to work, set hours, follow your direction for the team, attend recurring meetings at different times, and hold open houses, then they are said to be your employees. Therefore, you need to withhold income tax, social security, and report all earnings to the IRS. There might be extra responsibilities, such as auto insurance, healthcare, and office space.
- **Contractors.** Independent contractors work when they want to do it. Also, they provide their equipment and workspaces. If you're planning for contractors, you may pay them hourly or monthly.

Some responsibilities are better for employees, so make sure to consider what your requirements are before you post your job listing.

**Managing your real estate team.** Once your team is in place, you will need to manage your new employees to optimize your success. There are two powerful ways to do this: GPS tracking and tracking software.

**Don't wait to start expanding your team.** Creating a real estate team can be a powerful way to display more houses in a short period. Additionally, it can benefit your clients with more one-on-one attention.

If you're feeling the weight to work more just to fulfill client needs, now is the best time to invest in a team. It will be money well spent if you want to push your business to the next level.

**Where to Find Members of Your Real Estate Team**

There are many areas to find team members, but some best places to get started are asking other real estate investors. You can find other real estate investors by taking part in local real estate meetups, real estate groups on Facebook, or by requesting local real estate agents. Real estate investors work closely with the real estate investing team members you want to find as well. While you hunt for real estate investing team members, find out whether they have real estate investor friends in their network.

## Chapter 8: Real Estate Investment Strategies

Real estate is a big industry, and there are many opportunities to invest in real estate. But where can you start? What type of real estate investing is right for you? Mastering the ins and outs of how to invest in real estate is the first step in determining a strategy.

## Buy and Hold

The buy and hold real estate strategy is exactly as the name says. It is a way of buying an investment property to retain it for a long period of time-usually five years or more. So you're not buying, rehabbing, and instantly selling an investment property for a quick return. Although buy and hold real estate investors may want to sell their investment properties, that's more so down the line.

During the "holding" period, the investment property is erected as a rental. Renting out the property is where the profit on investment comes in. If the buy and hold real estate investment is done properly, you can gain from both short-term gains through positive cash flow and long term real estate appreciation.

This strategy is the best way to get started in real estate if you're a beginner. And that is because it is a straightforward method for first-time investors, unlike the fix-and-flip strategy, which demands experience to find the correct distressed properties. It's also the best strategy used by experienced property investors who want to create wealth over time from property appreciation and equity development.

**Buy and Hold Real Estate Types**

Rental properties are available in different sizes, shapes, and functions. To ensure that you are taking advantage of your buy and hold real estate technique, you need to decide the type of rental strategy you prefer.

Below are several income-generating assets you can invest in applying the buy and hold real estate investment method:

- **Turnkey real estate:** Investing in this type of property is when you buy a move-in ready property, which has professional property management and also has tenants already living in it. In other words, everything is taken care of. You only come to turn the key, and you will have a robust investment property.
- **Multi-family home:** We discussed this in the earlier chapters, but there is nothing to lose if we explain it further. It's a great choice for the buy and hold real estate investment strategy. A multi-family property refers to a building with more than one housing unit. They are more expensive than a single-family home. However, since you will be renting multiple units to multiple tenants, you will generate higher rental income. It is good for strong cash flow and quickly creating your investment portfolio.
- **Commercial real estate:** The buy and hold real estate investment method isn't just about residential real estate. Investors can also buy a property used for business purposes such as an office building or retail store. But commercial real estate investing could be more complex, especially for beginners.
- **Single-family homes:** This is combined with the traditional long-term rental strategy. You invest in a normal house and rent it out to a tenant. Many beginners prefer single-family homes as a means to get a feel of the real estate investing industry. A single rental unit and tenant to keep things

straightforward.

**Pros of Buy and Hold Real Estate Investment Method**

Besides the cash flow, there are many benefits to investing in buy and hold real estate:

1. **Rental income.** Why property investors go for a buy and hold real estate investment strategy is the monthly rental income. There could also be other channels of revenue, such as laundry, vending machines, and parking income. If you own a long term rental or include property management, all the generated revenue will be passive income, and you can confirm it every month.

2. **Tax deductions.** Rental expenses aren't all taxable. Apart from the property tax advantages, there are different expenses you can remove, like depreciation, loan origination fees, and mortgage interest. Other costs, such as maintenance and repairs, are tax-deductible.

3. **Appreciation.** Real estate appreciation is one of the best things that come out of the buy and hold real estate investment method. The real estate market can change after some years, but if you select a great city to buy and hold, your rental property will quickly skyrocket in value. Overall, buy and hold real estate appreciates at an annual rate between 3-5%.

4. **Equity.** When it comes to financing an investment property, it is done using bank loans. The best thing about the buy and hold real estate investment strategy is the tenants of your rental property may end up paying down your mortgage. While the rent that you collect clears the mortgage, the equity in your property increases every month. Tenants might even pay you interest costs. The secret here is to search for good tenants.

**Student Rental**

Investing in student rental is another real, profitable estate strategy. Buying a student housing property creates income as tenants pay rent, while also letting you gain from an increasing housing market. Student housing property investments are unique from other rental properties in different ways you should consider before buying.

**Choosing a Property**

Selecting the correct property is an important step to attain success in student rentals. Students always want to rent properties that are near public transit centers or campuses. In case there are numerous colleges in the area, determine the ones with high enrolments, since this will result in a higher demand for student housing. You will manage to request for a higher rent if your property is located in a safe neighborhood and has curb appeal. Other features that attract homeowners, such as newer kitchen and bath upgrades, may have little effect on what students are ready to pay for short-term leases.

**House Flipping**

Fix-and-flips are meant for investors searching for active short-term investments to generate money. They are properties that are purchased, improved, and then sold. These are not a get-rich-quick scheme, but if executed correctly, investors can profit from this strategy.

When you search for a house to flip, you should hunt for deal-breakers. Once you set a budget, it's vital to get in touch with an inspector, appraiser, and contractor to inspect for issues and avoid losing the money and time. When it comes to flipping houses, time is a great resource. The longer it takes to flip a house, the more monthly costs.

**Tips to Save You on Fix-And-Flip Repairs**

The success of a fix-and-flip investment strategy depends wholly on your potential to sell the rehabbed property at a price that not only reflects your total investment but also leaves you with a profit. However, if you are new to the real estate business, it's also easy to spend more than required on fix-and-flip repairs, and that can quickly decrease the amount of money you can make. Use the following tips to avoid making such mistakes:

1. **Adhere to your budget.** Let's say you used financing to buy the property, and you'll have assigned a given portion of the loan or secured an extra loan to cover the costs of fix-and-flip repairs. That sum should depend on the pre-purchase home inspection, as well as the contractor's analysis of the repair to be done and the expenses of labor and materials involved. If you apply this assessment as a foundation for each part of the rehab project, you'll avoid going over budget.
2. **Save on materials.** Make sure you manage the ordering and select materials yourself. If you allow your subcontractors to conduct this, it can cost more time.
3. **Use subcontractors.** The rates of subcontractors can go as high as 10 percent lower than contractors' rates. Ensure you employ subcontractors who are certified, and have enough experience. Additionally, reach an agreement in writing that states each party's rights and responsibilities.
4. **Special offers.** Search for special offers or seasonal discounts at typical hardware stores. You can still get a lot of discounts if you purchase at large scale suppliers.
5. **Salvage yards.** Remember to visit architectural salvage yards to identify unique items that add a touch of character to a property.

6. **Explore all shopping options.** If you want to save cash on the cost of materials, then you need to dig deep for deals. Go to lumber yards, yard sales, distributors, and even shop online.

7. **Gets hands-on.** The cost of labor has increased, so if there are repairs that you can do yourself to save money, why not try it.

## Why Fix-and-Flips Are One of the Best Investment Strategy

1. **Big profits.** The reason real estate investors go for a fix-and-flip is the profit. One of the best things about real estate flips is the opportunity to generate high profits in a very short period. This is why fix-and-flip is suitable for short-term real estate investment strategy.

2. **Gaining experience and knowledge faster.** Fixing and flipping real estate comprise of many transactions and operations that a real estate investor would require to address. This, however, presents a great opportunity to learn more about the real estate investing business. In the whole experience with real estate fix-and-flip, you'll manage to learn a lot about expenses, construction, budgeting, and the local real estate market.

3. **Forced appreciation.** Fix-and-flip is the best real estate investment strategy when it comes to fast appreciation. Once you buy the property and begin improving it, it increases in value. This is referred to as forced appreciation in real estate. Once you're done with the renovations, the property shoots up in the market value. Therefore, you can ask for a higher price that covers all the renovation costs plus having a huge profit margin with the deal.

4. **No big competition.** House flipping is a risky strategy. As such, not many people would like to risk with such a method. It sets less competition in the real estate market, which implies you have a higher opportunity of client turnout.

**Challenges of Investing in Fix-And-Flip Real Estate**

Before you step into a fix-and-flip, ensure you understand the following drawbacks:

**You invest more time and effort.** Investing in a fix-and-flip demands time and effort. Despite the advantages of being a short-term investment, you will be working full-time on it. First, you will take time before you get a property. You will also spend some time creating a budget and approximating the costs of repair as well as contacting handymen to do the work. Therefore, if you feel like you have the time and the energy to invest in a fix-and-flip real estate strategy, then go ahead. However, if you're a part-time investor, and is hard to set aside time, then it's better to choose other strategies.

**Unexpected costs.** While you will begin by approximating the repair costs, it doesn't mean that you will not have any unexpected expenses happening along the way. So, when investing in a fix-and-flip, you can never predict the types of costs that will happen unless you begin working on it.

**You have a time limit.** Flipping homes will put you in a time limit to sell the property. Otherwise, you will be risking additional property costs compounding and costing you your money. Therefore, the quicker you sell the property, the more you will save on property expenses. But to succeed in fix-and-flip, you must have great networking skills. Having networks has a big effect on your business, as you will always find amongst them someone who wants to buy a property.

If you're a beginner real estate investor, then it's better to go with low-risk investments first. Fix-and-flip is one of the high-risk real estate investment strategies.

**Short-Term Rental**

In recent years, short-term rental properties have become the best choice for tourists looking for temporary lodging while on holiday. They have also become a powerful way to invest in real estate. The financial advantages of owning an Airbnb property are clear to investors. Sometimes, they can even generate more money from short-term rentals than traditional long-term rentals.

Investing in short-term rentals can be an excellent experience, both for landlords and renters. The tenant, a tourist, gets to live in a homey environment without having to waste money on expensive restaurants. Overall, the rate for Airbnb rentals is lower than those for hotels. Additionally, landlords have a lot of advantages. They get to learn about different cultures and traditions from different tourists without having to leave their homes. Also, they enjoy the high cash on a return that their property generates.

Below are tips to remember before deciding to invest in short-term rentals:

**Understand the regulations regarding short-term rentals.** Before you even decide to rent your property using short-term rental sites such as Airbnb, you need to learn more about your city and state laws about Airbnb rentals. Airbnb regulations differ from city to city and are changing every day. That is the reason you must keep yourself updated on short-term guidelines to make sure you don't fall into anything illegal.

In certain states and cities, more rigid laws and regulations are applied to Airbnb rentals.

**Determine the costs.** If you don't factor the total costs that come with your real estate investment strategy, you may end up struggling with a negative cash flow property instead of enjoying the positive cash flow. With short-term rentals, if you forget to include electricity in your costs can eat your profit and leave you with losses. You have to factor all the expenses related to your property. Some critical costs to consider include:

- Airbnb cleaning fee of around $50 per booking
- Suppliers estimated at $150
- Utilities of about $200
- Monthly mortgage payment

Computing costs can be a big headache. It is easy to compute your related rental costs by using an Airbnb profitability calculator. This tool determines the viability of an Airbnb investment property.

**Select the right location.** One thing that cannot change in real estate investing, no matter your investment strategy, is the significance of the location. Some locations are better for traditional rentals, and others generate higher profits for short-term rental properties. It is your responsibility to study and analyze the real estate market to find out which rental strategy is the best.

To find the best places for Airbnb properties, investors base on specific factors like affordability, occupancy rate, potential ROI, and short-term rental rates. For example, places with plenty of tourist attractions such as a national park and beaches are the first choice for Airbnb investors. These are better locations; hence, the occupancy rate and demand for short-term rental properties are high.

However, before you proceed to purchase a vacation home rental, you need to confirm whether these areas have positive investment potential.

Whatever your city of choice for investing in short-term rental properties, you will still need to search for a profitable neighborhood.

**Identify the perfect property.** Selecting a profitable short-term rental property demands the same amount of due diligence to identify profitable traditional rentals. Once you are sure in your location, the next thing is to select the kind of vacation rental property to purchase. Popular types include single-family homes, condos, and multi-family properties. Every type of investment property has unique features that attract short-term guests.

In summary, there is a huge potential to earn money from short-term rental properties. You don't need to have a foundation in real estate investing to become successful, but it can take time to become successful.

Besides that, vacation home rentals can generate high profits but will also have high costs tied with them.

For that reason, we recommend starting slow and researching enough before getting started. Allow yourself to determine what works and what doesn't, what mistakes to avoid, and what seems to click with Airbnb guests.

**Turnkey Investing**

A turnkey property refers to a fully refurbished apartment building that an investor can buy and immediately rent out. A turnkey property is a property bought from a company that focuses on the restoration of old properties. The same companies may also offer property management to buyers to cut down on the amount of time and effort they have to put into the rental.

The acquisition of turnkey property is expected to let the new buyer allow tenants to enter immediately. By buying real estate that requires no repair, the focus is to rent the property as quickly as possible. The level of work required to convert a property into a turnkey condition may include repairs of plumbing, replacement of electrical fixtures, and fixes to the flooring where relevant. The shorter the time it takes to rent the property, the faster the new buyer may begin to enjoy the profit of their investment.

## Chapter 9: Long-Distance Real Estate Investment

If you are starting in the real estate business, most successful property investors will tell you to invest where you live. This is nice advice because it's difficult to gain deep knowledge of a real estate market if you're not living there. For an experienced real estate investor considering expanding his or her portfolio, long-distance real estate investing is a good option. If you have any questions that this method works, think about the fact that many multi-millionaires generated wealth through owning commercial and residential investment properties across the world. Well, how can you start to generate money with long-distance real estate investing?

**First, research the real estate market.** The location will always be a critical factor that affects your investment decisions. There are specific elements that make a place attractive for owning an investment property, such as a stable economy, population growth, and job opportunities. Therefore, if you're thinking about long-distance real estate investing, you have to conduct your research to get the right location that provides these elements.

Also, property investors need to stay current with market trends such as regulations and laws, interest rates, property taxes, etc. Analyze what your target tenants are searching for to determine what the best rental property in the place looks like and in which neighborhoods people are migrating. In general, perform your research to determine the best location for long-distance real estate investing.

**Focus on the numbers.** Becoming a member of the real estate club means you need to perform some computations before you decide anything. While you're studying the real estate market where you want to invest, review the odds of return of rental properties in that given market based on cash return, occupancy rate, and positive cash flow. Don't run the numbers only on the rental property you are targeting; you also need to understand how these numbers fit into the housing market. In other words, conduct a real estate market analysis.

This is essential because you want to ensure that long-distance real estate investing is worthy, and more attractive than your local housing market. Additionally, if you are thinking about how to rent out your investment property, these numbers will allow you to know the type of rental strategy that generates a better profit on investment.

**Apply real estate investment tools.** The current technology is the major contributor to making long-distance real estate investing a viable option. Nowadays, property investors can easily access online tools that allow them to acquire all the information they need about real estate. An example of such a tool is the investment property calculator. The tool provides projections of what cash on cash return, rental income, and many more you can expect. Therefore, a real estate investor can review and compare different locations in the comfort of his/her home.

Also, other real estate investment tools help you search for and find properties online.

**Think about getting a real estate partner.** Even with the help of online tools, long-distance real estate investing is still difficult. Maybe you want to buy an investment property in a country or city that you cannot access for one reason or another. In the following case, getting a partner is the most convenient solution. Also, real estate partnerships are great because they generate resources, including experience, networking, knowledge, and capital. Not forgetting to say, they can decrease the general risk of investing in real estate. Therefore, having a partner can simplify your life as a real estate investor.

**Get a professional property management company.** With long-distance real estate investing, comes the question of how to control rental properties that are far away. If you are not interested in getting a partner in the city you want to invest in, then your other channel is to allow a property management company to handle the business. These companies will everything, including checking on the investment property, tenant screening, conducting relevant repairs, etc. Remember, a professional property management company comes with a fee. Therefore, property investors should look for the best company they can trust with their real estate properties.

## Key Problems of Long-Distance Real Estate Investing

1. Owning an investment property out of state is tiresome if a real estate investor doesn't have enough experience in and knowledge related to real estate investing.
2. There will be a time lag in realizing changes in the real estate market and noticing the nuances of change that may signal the need to sell your investment property before problems arrive.
3. Investing in out of state real estate market is more difficult to handle than in a local market, and it's also very expensive.
4. Hiring the wrong person to manage your property could be a big problem. Real estate investors have to trust others to look after their rental properties.
5. Failing to invest time and enough research analyzing the housing market, the location, and the neighborhood before purchasing the rental property may result in huge losses.

**Tips for a Profitable Long-Distance Real Estate Investing**

1. **Get your finances in order first.** The most common misconception in real estate is the idea of investing with no cash. This is typically not true, and if you are planning to invest far from the state, you must have the financial capability to buy and manage. Ensure you have enough savings if you want to try long-distance real estate investing and reap huge profits in the long run.

2. **Evaluate the worthiness of long-distance real estate investing.** Get the right real estate investment deal that generates high returns. The ROI in long-distance real estate investing must be significant and more lucrative than your local housing market. If you can get a similar real estate deal generating similar returns in your local housing market, it is only reasonable to invest where you live. However, if the chance to invest out of state has advantages and is worth the chase, then go for it.

3. **Watch out for state laws regarding real estate investors and landlords.** The main purpose of long-distance real estate investing is to get a nice ROI and earn high profits in return. Before you dive in on investment property, ensure you pay attention to the State Laws and property taxes regarding your real estate business. If the taxes are too high, they may eat into your profits and make long-distance real estate investing bad news for your bottom line.

4. **Search for trends of the market present and future.** You should adapt to the housing market conditions and general trends of where you want to invest. Successful real estate investors perform a lot of research and market analysis before they take advantage of the right location. Without investing in the right location, investors will not reap the highest advantages and rewards of real estate, especially in the long-distance real estate investing.

5. **Do not discount the price to rent ratio.** One of the easiest ways to take

advantage of the location for real estate investing is to apply the price to rent ratio across different real estate markets to determine the capitalization rate, the occupancy rate, and the rental income. The price to rent ratio provides real estate investors with a great idea of where to purchase real estate for profit.

6. **Determine the correct professional property management team.** This is a critical factor in long-distance real estate investing. Invest in the right people and the right professional property management team to run your real estate properties on your behalf. Treat real estate such as business, and place a high value in selecting the best people to run your business.

7. **Deep research, analysis, and being informed.** Don't crunch numbers only on the investment property you are planning. Analyze your profit potential and approximate how your prospective investment numbers suit the local housing market.

8. **Gain enough experience and knowledge before diving in long-distance real estate investing.** Again, if you're buying your first investment property, it is important to invest where you live. As you gain experience and gain the right knowledge, you can branch out and consider long-distance real estate investing in expanding your real estate investment portfolio.

9. **Define clear-cut processes.** When you've developed a local real estate investing business, you can make up for a lot of half-assed processes. You can speak to tenants one-on-one, drive to the property if you want, or rush to the title company, and you can even try to fix things yourself. However, when you own a long-distance real estate investing company, your processes must be clear and systematic. The better your means for finding tenants, collaborating with your property management company, and getting contractors, the easier it will be running your business.

Don't cut corners, and don't leave a bad process to fend for itself. It might cost you time and money in the long run, and it may even topple your business if you aren't careful.

**Is Long-Distance Real Estate Investing Business Right for You?**

You understand the pros and cons of building a long-distance real estate investing business. You also understand the advanced steps to build one. The only thing left is to determine whether long-distance real estate investing business is right for you. Or would you prefer to establish a local business?

The choice is yours.

The great thing about real estate investing is that there is no one-way road to success and riches. Tech-savvy real estate investors discover creative ways to real estate investing to earn long-term financial rewards and high ROI on their real estate investments. If implemented properly, long-distance real estate investing can be a very lucrative real estate opportunity with better returns than your local market.

Lastly, don't limit your investment opportunities. But one thing for sure, perform your due diligence and monitor the housing market before you jump all in.

## Chapter 10: How to Finance Your Real Estate Transaction

One of the major problems that beginner investors experience when they decide to take part in real estate investing is discovering the best source of financing. Many avoid investing in properties because they have little or no cash to put down.

However, the biggest misconception about real estate investing is that you need to have more money to get started. The lack of enough money to make a down payment continues to prevent many beginner investors in the current market. The fact that many people don't know is that there are different alternative real estate investment financing methods perfect for beginners.

As a newbie investor, understanding how to get financing for a real estate investment is very important. How a given real estate deal is financed can also influence its results.

### Conventional Mortgages

A conventional mortgage is the most popular financing method for real estate investing. To find one, you need to make a certain down payment, and then the bank loans you with the remaining cash. Although conventional mortgages have a lower interest rate, they follow a tight deadline. You need to have enough down payments, a good credit score, and a low debt-to-income ratio. These requirements can limit some investors.

Conventional mortgages are the best for buy and hold investors who want to develop a real estate portfolio of income properties. The mortgage repayments are always done every month, making them easier to budget for. However, these loans aren't the best for short-term financing.

**Real Estate Partnerships**

Real estate partnerships are a great real estate investment financing option for first-time investors. You can look for somebody with enough money for a down payment and collaborate with them. For example, you can partner with a family member or a friend who wants to take part in real estate investment but doesn't want to be involved in the daily work of managing a rental property. Your partner will handle all the financial risk, and you will do all the groundwork of generating rental income. What your partner lacks is made up for by you.

To succeed in a real estate partnership, both of you need to reach an agreement on how the profits will be shared. Also, put all the terms you agree on in writing, including the responsibilities of all parties.

**Things You Need to Do to Make a Real Estate Partnership Succeed**

**Select the right investment partner.** Finding the right individual to partner with is the first critical aspect of establishing a real estate partnership. This is a person you will be spending a lot of time with. As a result, you must partner with someone you like and know very well. If you haven't had a chance to work or interact with them before, consider trying out one or two deal with them to understand how they work. If your first project fails, it will be easier to move on.

Learning how to search for real estate investors is important if you want to have a successful real estate partnership. Spend time to screen your partner to make sure they are a good fit. A good real estate partner should access enough capital, have important connections, and boast of complementary skills. Conduct thorough research to determine your prospective partner's experience, credibility, and track record–request for references where possible.

You can find real estate investors from friends and family, your real estate network, and real estate investment groups.

**Have common objectives.** Another important aspect of a successful real estate partnership is making sure that you and your partner have common objectives. Select a partner that has a similar mindset towards real estate investing as you. What is the level of return do you expect? What real estate investment strategies do you want to apply? For how long do you want to be in the business? If your prospective partner has a similar objective to yours, then there could be a great foundation to create a real estate partnership. While it's not necessary to agree on everything, you should ensure that you share primary goals. This will help both of you in building a business plan, which will be your roadmap to success.

**A real estate partnership agreement.** Everything you and your partner agree must be represented in writing. Make sure you draft and sign a real estate partnership agreement between you and your partner. The presence of an agreement helps to make things clear in case of legal issues in the future or when the real estate partners choose to divide up. It acts as a security for both partners. Even when your partnership is with a family member or friend, a partnership contract is necessary.

The agreement represents the responsibilities assigned to every partner, how the profits will be divided, the steps for resolving disputes, what happens when a partner becomes incapacitated, or wishes to end the partnership.

**Good communication.** Communication is vital for any partnership in real estate. Constant communication allows a person to build trust between partners. To establish a long-lasting, successful collaboration, you need to develop open and honest communication. Regular check-ins with your partner on the state of affairs should be performed and ensure that both of you are still aligned with your goals for the business. You can have weekly or monthly reviews on your goals to make sure you are working towards a common target.

In cases there are any issues, it is important to raise them as soon as they pop up. Practically, discussing problems as soon as they occur can help prevent bigger problems in the future, which can be devastating to your business. Solve any problems that arise and refine the agreement to ensure such problems don't happen again.

**Real estate investment tools.** Real estate investing is a competitive business. The returns of the real estate partnership will highly depend on the investment properties you get. Searching for real estate investment opportunities requires a person to identify the best location and conduct the correct analysis of investment properties in the area to determine the most profitable ones.

A real estate partnership should take advantage of real estate investment tools to find the most profitable investments in the market that are under the objectives.

**Seller Financing**

This type of real estate investment financing requires that you receive a loan from the property seller. In case the property seller is ready to present you with a loan, this can be a great choice for beginners. Seller financing is easy to get and requires less paperwork than a conventional mortgage from a bank. Seller financing deals work in different ways. The seller can finance either the down payment for an investment property or the total buying price. To be successful, make sure you and the seller agree on a fair interest rate for your loan. Also, ensure that you state all the terms of the loan in writing and sign it.

## Federal Housing Administration Loan

If you're buying your first investment property, then FHA loans could help you own the property. The FHA loan was created to support homeownership. But you can purchase a multifamily property using a down payment of only 3.5%, choose one unit to live in and rent out the rest to qualify. This makes an FHA loan a cost-effective real estate investment financing plan, especially if it's your first.

## Private Money Lenders

Private money lenders are a powerful real estate investment financing option for new investors. They are nonprofessional individuals who lend property loans at a given interest rate and payback interval. They are normally interested in investing in the property just like you are.
If you are well-connected, you make use of capital from your network. This could be a friend, co-worker, etc. private money loans require little qualifications than conventional loans and have a flexible loan structure. These loans are commonly attained by real estate investors who believe they can increase the value of an investment property over a short period using repairs.

## Home Equity Loan

This is a real estate investment financing approach where the lender uses your existing property as security for the loan. It helps you to take advantage of your already existing equity. But, you risk facing foreclosures and losing your home if you don't keep up with monthly payments. Make sure you measure the risk before deciding to use this option. Home equity loans are provided by banks and other financial companies.

**Hard Money Lenders**

Traditional mortgage normally lasts around 60 days before closing. This is a long period if you are making a deal. Hard money lenders solve this problem. Hard money loans serve on a short-term basis. They are always backed by the property value.

While hard money loans have higher interest rates, they provide you with the flexibility to strike fast when you have a great deal in your hands. It might not be a sustainable long-term real estate investment financing choice. But it's a great resource when you want to close quickly. These loans are used as bridge loans to help close a deal before you earn traditional financing.

In summary, the main challenge beginner real estate investors face getting capital. But, there are different ways to finance a real estate investment even if you don't have the cash. Even so, not all real estate investment financing options are similar. Each choice has its own set of cons and pros. The real estate financing approach you apply will depend on the investment property and your unique financial situation.

## Chapter 11: Mortgages

Stable housing prices and low-interest rates in traditional investment products has driven interest in investing in various types of real estate securities. Mortgage investment entities (MIE), such as the mortgage pool or mortgage investment corporation, are great examples of real estate investments that have witnessed growth in recent years. These securities are always sold with the hope of stable and enticing annual returns of 6-10%, which has attracted the interest of investors searching for higher yields.

Not all MIEs are the same. Some have different structures, fees, and risks that you need to understand and carefully consider before investing. Investing in private MIEs is risky, and you should not invest unless you can afford to lose all the cash you paid for the investment.

Mortgages for Real Estate

In general, when investors need mortgage financing to purchase a home or a commercial property, they borrow from convention lending sources like credit unions and banks. For those individuals that aren't able to find a loan from these traditional sources, they always resort to alternative types of mortgage lenders. The private lenders may include mortgage investment entities or MIEs.

An MIE is a mortgage-financing business that collects money from investors to lend people as mortgages. Mortgages are protected by real property such as a piece of land, house, or a strip mall, but the MIE investor doesn't own a part of that land or home.

Adjustable-Rate Mortgage (ARM)

An adjustable-rate lease refers to the type of mortgage where the interest rate applied on the remaining balance differs throughout the life of the loan. With an adjustable-rate mortgage, the price of interest is fixed for a given time, after which it resets periodically, usually every year or even monthly.

A variable rate mortgage or VRM has an interest rate reset depending on a benchmark or index, as well as additional spread.

Things are more complicated for the real estate investor with the adjustable-rate mortgage. The lender will provide you with the money and mortgage the property at an adjustable interest rate.

Adjustable vs. Fixed-Rate Mortgages

When you receive a mortgage, there are many loan features to consider. One of the significant factors is whether to use a fixed or adjustable-rate mortgage. Each has drawbacks and benefits, and your budget, housing requirements, and appetite for risk will be a significant factor in your decision.

Balloon Mortgage

When you buy a property with a balloon mortgage, you will start to make monthly payments for an amount that is close to a standard 30-year fixed mortgage at the same rate.

However, after 5-7 years, you will stop regular monthly payments and pay off the rest of the balance. In other words, a balloon mortgage is a short-term loan structured like a long-term loan for the first few years.

Government-Insured Mortgages

Government mortgage programs such as USDA, FHA, and VA can help prospective investors to purchase rental properties for a low down payment. For example, FHA loans can have a down payment as low as 3.5%. Other program types can also result in reduced down payments.

## Chapter 12: Exit Strategy and 1031 Exchanges

Many people join the real estate investing business for the financial advantages this market provides. There's no secret that the entire reason for buying investment properties is to generate income through appreciation in the years to come. No successful real estate investor gets into the market without having a strong business model. Therefore, having an exit strategy before even buying a real estate investment property is crucial.

### What Is a Real Estate Exit Strategy?

This is a way in which an investor plans to close a real estate deal. Different exit strategies are planned by real estate investors. Some investors start to plan for an exit strategy when they have a clear understanding of the investment.

But the best advice for real estate investors is to have an exit strategy before buying an investment property.

Normally, property investors fail to understand the need to have an exit strategy when looking for a real estate deal. So, why are exit strategies so important?

### The Benefit of Real Estate Exit Strategy

Various reasons may drive real estate investors into implementing an exit strategy:

- Determining the correct real estate exit strategy not only will provide real estate investors with a plan of action, but it will also reduce incoming risks. When property investors examine possible exit strategies before buying investment properties, they understand the risks connected with the investment and how to avoid them.

- A specific exit strategy is crucial to success, as the right approach will lead to optimized profits. It's never wise to get into real estate investing without having a clear picture of how you will gain from the real estate property when closing the deal. For that reason, a financial goal and exit strategy can save you thousands, if not millions of dollars throughout your real estate investing career.

- Suppose you buy an investment property, and later, you realize that real estate investing isn't your thing. Or, if you cannot keep up with the demands of the real estate investment market or have lost your knack and now your real estate property is becoming an obstacle. There are reasons why having a closing strategy before investing in properties is important.

- Unexpected emerges can affect anyone. An investor might get stuck by an accident and in desperate need of money. In the following case, a real estate exit strategy is critical to sell the property faster and cash out.

- Real estate exit strategies are also important for investors who are planning to grow their real estate investment portfolios and have large investments. This is perhaps one of the most common reasons to execute an exit strategy because it will provide property investors knowledge of how to control these different investment properties and to respond in case one of them isn't generating a return based on rental income appreciation.

**Best Real Estate Exit Strategies**

Understanding and selecting the correct exit strategy will affect how successful you will be in your real estate investing career.

**Fix-and-flip strategy:** This strategy results in the highest profit because it allows the real estate investor to sell the real estate property at total market value. It involves buying investment properties that require repair and then selling them for more than the original investment costs.

Remember that real estate investors who want to implement this strategy should know of market trends, and capable of quickly adding value to real estate investment properties.

Not every property qualifies for a good flip, though. Confirm your property is in a good location, and that it has great amenities before you start to renovate.

You don't need to go into detail in every room, but you must pay special attention to the bathrooms and kitchen. These rooms tend to drive buyers one way or the other, and you will receive your money back.

Next, you can implement your exit strategy_ you can sell your flip and repay the costs of repair and other property-related costs in the sale.

**Buy and Hold:** This strategy is common for real estate investors who want to grow equity in a real estate property. It resembles a fix-and-flip, instead of selling the improved property, the investor decides to hold it for a while and rent it out to receive monthly cash flow. While appreciation and equity develop, these investment properties can be sold for a profit.

**Seller Financing Deal:** Probably, you have a tenant who wants to stay in your property even though you want to sell it. In this case, you can sign a seller financing deal if the person is interested in buying the property themselves. The biggest advantage of this strategy is the amount you will save on real estate commissions and listing your home. The deal will be completed, and you only need to solidify the terms.

The whole transaction revolves around a promissory note, where you include how your tenant will repay you the property. You will agree on a monthly payment and interest rate, plus any required down payment. This model provides you with another advantage because they'll be paying you rent plus interest every month. You will still generate cash from your rental property. Once the deal is over, the seller financing deal replaces the typical landlord duties from your shoulders. Now, the tenant becomes the technical owner, and they're responsible for paying incidentals.

Finally, should anything wrong happen, you have the house as collateral. You get it back if they fail to pay. There's only one critical thing, and it's that you must own your home before you set up such a deal. Or else, you have to notify your lender of your plan, and they have to approve it.

**Traditional Selling with a Real Estate Agent**

In this approach, you buy a property and later sell it using a real estate agent for a higher price. Real estate investors depending on this technique, will fund the property themselves or deal with a mortgage lender. This strategy is attractive because of its simplicity. However, investors who don't purchase the best market could experience high holding costs and small profit margins. The level of profit of a buy and sell deal will depend wholly on the buying price of the property. To make the best profit, investors should research on motivated sellers, the best markets, and negotiation tips.

**1031 Exchanges**

The 1031 exchange refers to the application of the section 1031 of the United States Internal Revenue Code, and it helps real estate investors to make the most out of their investments by swapping one investment property for another similar property.

When it comes to real estate investing, the 1031 exchange has a very simple implementation to boost your revenue and profits while eliminating the quick taxes that may apply to your investment and reduce your profits.

In simple terms, 1031 exchange lets an investor dispose of his/her asset and attain a similar asset before generating a tax liability from selling the first asset.

In short, what a real estate investor can benefit from a 1031 exchange is to buy a starter property, and after several years, once the property has generated return, and increased in value, the real estate investor can sell the property and use the cash from the sale of the property to buy another large investment property.

Successful investors go for this approach to keep expanding their business overtime while avoiding paying taxes on the sale of every property they own. They continue selling properties and buying better ones, effectively increasing their investment business and growing it over the years.

**How to Select the Best Exit Strategy?**

The decision to choose one of the above exit strategies is not as simple as it may appear. There is no rule to differentiate between them. Additionally, there are different factors to consider when planning an exit strategy. Mastering these factors will let a real estate investor determine the real estate strategy he or she should follow.

**Factors That Could Affect an Exit Strategy**

It's critical for a real estate investor to understand that specific factors may destroy a planned real estate exit strategy, such as:

- Depreciation

- Poor property management that decreases the value and possible cash flow
- Tenant problems in lost rent
- Unexpected maintenance costs

Successful real estate investors can overcome these potential challenges by having multiple exit strategies. Things can change at any given time, which is why you need to have a backup plan.

Before you make a real estate investing deal and buy investment properties, real estate investors should understand the means to get out of the investment property and when to sell it to make a profit. This is the whole point of real estate investing. An exit strategy is a means to let the real estate investor to cash out of the investment property with minimum problems.

With the above exit strategies, a real estate investor can walk away from rental property with pride. Not only will you release yourself of what has become a financial burden, but you can do so in the most profitable fashion.

# Conclusion

For many years, property investment has been the most popular way of building wealth across the globe. It is a million-dollar debate on which is better: real estate or stocks?

When implemented the right way, real estate investing can generate high returns through rental income, tax benefits, and the capital appreciation gained from buying below market value.

However, real estate investing is not for everyone. It takes time to master real estate investing. It takes perseverance and effort to discover great deals and even more financial discipline to save enough cash to get moving.

The positive side of big profits isn't necessarily to say that you cannot benefit from the current market. And there are many reasons to suggest that waiting is going to affect your investment portfolio negatively.

It might be years until the next market downturn or hope for steady economic growth, which may never happen.

If you wait for that long, you will be missing out on a time where you could be getting your money to work for you. Rather than get more cash and asset-rich in readiness for the next market crash, you will just be sitting on cash, waiting.

Investing in real estate may appear like something only the rich people can do. But everyday investors can always invest in real estate too. You may not buy a multi-million-dollar apartment structure, but you can invest in a starter home, transparent mortgages, and then rent it for a profit once you purchase your next home.

But real estate can be a bit complex and tricky than just buying mutual funds using 401(k). So, while everyday investors can put money into real estate, you should not do so until you exactly know what you're doing.

Getting started in real estate is made easy with *Real Estate Investing for Beginners*. After reading this comprehensive guide, you are now ready to become a real estate investor. The sooner you start, the sooner you will begin to earn money and enjoy success.

Finally, if you found this book useful in any way, a review on Amazon is always appreciated!

# Dropshipping Shopify E-Commerce Business Model

*The Ultimate Step by Step Guide on How to Create a Passive Income Cash Flow, Make Money Online from Home and Achieve Financial Freedom*

*Brandon J. Swing*

# Table of Contents

# Introduction

Building a business is certainly not easy. In fact, it can seem quite daunting and scary; however, I want to congratulate you on taking the first step – that is making your mind up about starting your own business. There are several perks of being an entrepreneur and you can reap all of them if you know what you need to do. Don't be under any misconception about the effort and time it takes to launch a business and make it successful. You need to be willing to dedicate the necessary time and effort. After all, Rome wasn't built in a day. So, if you think that you can launch a successful business overnight, you need to think again.

If you want to start a dropshipping business and earn passive income, then this is the perfect book for you. In this book, you will learn everything that you need to know about successfully launching your dropshipping business. You will learn about the benefits of passive income, the meaning of dropshipping, steps to launch a dropshipping business, and the ways to make your business successful.

Dropshipping is one of the best means of earning passive income and once you are armed with all the knowledge provided in this book, you can attain all your financial goals.

Passive income can help you to earn some extra money or even substitute your regular income. The capital you decide to invest can be as high or as low as you want it to be. There are no hard and fast rules about passive earnings! You are your boss, and it can be fun!

So, if you are ready to learn more about all this, then let us start without further ado.

## Chapter 1: Passive Income and Its Benefits

Why does everyone chase the idea of passive income? There are plenty of benefits that passive income offers that regular business options don't. If you want to increase your wealth, then your source of income must not just be your 9-5 job. Instead, you must focus on setting up a system of passive income. In this section, you will learn about the different benefits that passive income offers.

### You Are Your Boss

If you work a 9-5 job, then you will have a boss. You will be responsible for your boss for every activity that you undertake at your workplace. Therefore, there will be a limit on the freedom that you have while you execute a task. You cannot do things on your terms, and you will always be answerable to someone. There is a strict hierarchy that you have to follow. All this restrains your creativity and doesn't let you excel. When it comes to a passive income business, you are your boss. There aren't any restrictions on what you do when you work, or how you work. When you work for others, you have to follow their rules. When you work for yourself, you can create your own rules. You can be as creative as you want, and you can establish your standards.

### Less Scope for Mediocrity

In a company, more often than not, most people tend to do mediocre work. Mediocrity creeps in when you have to do something that you don't want to do. For instance, if you have to complete a task within two hours, some might take up to five hours or more to do the same work. If the average working hours are 8 hours per day and they work on a task for two hours, then they don't have anything to do for the other 6 hours. On the other hand, they will get more work if they complete one task. Therefore, they might postpone one job to limit their workload. All these reasons make the company's environment mediocre instead of productive. The passive income business is your venture, and your interests are the only ones that are involved. Therefore, you will give it your best shot. Regardless of tiredness, you feel at the end of the day, the job satisfaction you receive makes up for the rest. Since it is your brainchild, you will give it your best.

**Work Environment**

As mentioned in the previous point, the work environment in a company nurtures mediocrity. If everyone around you does mediocre work, then so will you. The circle you maintain has a startling effect on your life. If you want to be successful, you must surround yourself with successful people. When you opt for a passive income business, you can either choose your pack members or work as a lone wolf. You don't have to work with someone forcefully. When you can select your team or your partners by yourself, you can avoid mediocrity. You can instead opt for those who bring out the best in you.

**Taxes**

The income you earn from a regular job is taxable. The rate of taxation differs from one country to another. However, all posts are taxed at a certain percentage. One thing you can be sure of is that the taxes payable on the income you earn from a passive income business aren't as high as the ones applicable to your regular job. Hire the services of a professional accountant, and you can further reduce the taxes payable.

**Vacation Time**

If you work for someone, you will need their approval before you can go on leave. You need to submit a leave application and then wait for its sanction before you can take a holiday. If you do choose a leave, there is a loss of pay involved as well. You certainly cannot go on a month-long vacation while you work. However, when it comes to a passive income business, you can take leave whenever you want to. Your work can travel with you. So, all those beach holidays you promised yourself can finally come true! All that you need to monitor your business are a laptop and a good Internet connection. If you have these two things, you can do business from anywhere in the world. You can work at your convenience. A conventional job wouldn't let you work from anywhere. But now that your store is online, you can work from anywhere. You don't even have to worry about office space.

## No Office Politics

You are responsible for all the decisions you make about the business. You don't have to impress your boss or worry about your colleagues anymore. Your opinion is the only one that matters, along with the view of your target audience. You don't have to convince anyone of the idea you have. If you think your idea is profitable, then go ahead and implement it. It provides you complete autonomy of operations.

## No Pink Slips

Since you are your boss, you no longer have to worry about pink slips. No one can fire you. You don't have to live under the constant fear of being fired. You wouldn't find yourself devoid of any work. Once you establish your source of passive income, you can start to earn the returns it offers with minimal work. Passive income generates money continually. There isn't a retirement age in this field, and you can work for as long as you want to.

**Your Preferences Matter**

With a passive income business, you can do what you enjoy. You don't have to sit in a cubicle all day long doing things that you don't enjoy. Instead, you can make the most of your creativity and put it to better use. You can transform your hobby or passion into a passive income business. It depends on your ability to apply yourself. You don't have to sit around for hours and work on a boring presentation, just because your boss asked you to!

## Chapter 2: Work Ethic

Perhaps the most straightforward way you can gain financial independence is to reprogram your life in such a way that a significant portion of your income doesn't arise from active labor. Instead, it comes from passive income. The basic idea of passive income is that it refers to the money you receive with little effort, once you successfully create your source of income. There are different sources from which you can earn passive income. Some of the most popular sources are rent from real estate, royalties from patents, royalties from books, dividends from stocks, interest on other securities, affiliate marketing, and so on.

Is passive income a myth or a miracle? In fact, it is a combination of both. We can all safely agree that money indeed doesn't grow on trees and the concept of free lunch doesn't exist. What does the phrase "passive income" make you feel? There are different views about passive income and with all the views comes a lot of confusion. Quick and easy riches are what one thinks about when they hear the phrase "passive income." However, for it to be true, you must put in the necessary effort and gather all the knowledge required. Since the concept of passive income is widely misunderstood, let us first understand what passive income means.

Passive income is a form of business that has developed a process that caters to the daily requirements of business so that the owner doesn't have to. It means that certain aspects of the business can run smoothly without the need to monitor it continuously. It is a recurring stream of revenue that doesn't need the constant hands-on involvement of its creator. As a business owner, you can generate passive income only after you invest enough time and effort to create a valuable product along with automated systems to keep the business going. Passive income helps you to leverage your time in such a manner that you can create a more significant impact and help your business grow as well. During the initial stages, you must invest a lot of time in your business and create products that provide some value to customers. Passive income offers plenty of benefits that go beyond financial freedom. The streams of income you set up can help you make the most of your time, passion, creativity, as well as energy. Once you create an automated system that will scale your business, you will have plenty of time to do something else that you enjoy. It means that you can step away from your mundane work life and work on things that provide you with job satisfaction as well as a source of income. A substantial benefit that passive income offers is that it allows you the time to start other passive income businesses as well. Once your first business is up and running, you can start another one.

One thing that you must be aware of is that passive income isn't entirely passive. Certain aspects of it are passive. However, it isn't possible to run a successful business that passive. Regardless of its efficiency or the experience you possess, there will always be certain overheads that you have to take care of, update different aspects of the business, work on expanding the audience pool, and so on. The concept of a business that is entirely hands-free just doesn't exist.

Maintenance of some form or the other lives in every business. Passive income isn't about finding a way to generate income without any work, and the misconception that it is a hands-off job are the two main reasons for the failure of most passive income ventures. You cannot create something, ignore it, and then expect it to flourish. Nothing on this earth works like that. If you don't water the plant, the plant will die, even if it is a cactus. The same logic applies to your business as well.

## Why Do a Lot of Passive Income Businesses Fail?

The inherent flaw of all failed passive income businesses is the attitude of the creator. If the primary focus of the business is to quickly walk away and stop working on the business, then the business will never get the opportunity it needs to be successful. It takes dedication, passion, and hard work to run a business. If your main aim is to make a quick buck, then your business will miss out on a lot of opportunities that are essential for its success. Here are the aspects of a business that you need to focus on:

### Customers

If you want to work towards a passive income business, then the one aspect of the business you must not forget is your customers. Customers need to know that you care about them and you need to earn their trust. They need to know that your business will cater to their needs. A loyal customer base can establish your authority as well as credibility. As soon as customers feel that you are not in it for the long haul, they will turn to a business that is. If earning money is your only objective, then it will show. If you don't believe in what you are offering, then your customer will not believe in it either. If you don't have any customers, then who will you sell your products to? So, you need to work hard to establish a loyal customer base for your business.

### Competition

You need to remember that you are not the only player in the market. If you want to be a successful business owner, then you need to keep up with your competitors. You need to update yourself with new trends. Not just that, you also need to do some research about the factors that motivate the customer to opt for other brands. You need to make it a point to keep up with your competitors as well as the industry. If you think you can run your business without doing all this, then you are sadly mistaken.

## The Right Mindset

You need to have the right business mindset if you want to build a successful passive income business. In fact, before you start any business you need to ensure that your motivations point you towards creating value for your customers. Is money your only motivation? Are you considering passive income only for personal gain? Are you going to make someone else pull all your weight and then take credit for it? If your answer is yes, then you can't become a successful passive income earner. If you want to earn money and see growth, then you need to focus on creating value for your customers. You will be in the trenches for a while and you will need to put in all the necessary hard work. You must remember that nothing worth having ever comes easy. You need to be passionate about your work and you must be willing to work hard to achieve your professional goals. If you want to be successful, then you need to create a value-centric, customer loving, and focused mindset at work.

## Good Work Ethics

Success cannot be attained overnight; it needs a lot of hard work and effort. A successful business owner knows this and is willing to put in the necessary efforts. It takes time, effort, work, and discipline to create a business that will help you earn passive income. You need to have the drive and the motivation to make all this come true.

## No Accountability

Having business accountability is important. When you decide to start a business by yourself, you are not accountable to anyone except yourself. No one is there to notice whether you show up for work or not, if you work hard, or even crack a new business deal. It is important that you can hold yourself accountable for the way you carry on with your business. Self-accountability isn't easy to enforce, and it is something that you need to do intentionally. Self-guilt stems from self-accountability, and you must be strong enough to deal with it. You can always approach others to make you more accountable. You can approach your friend and make sure that you aren't spiraling out of control or heading towards a meltdown. When you are the owner of a business, all the important decisions rest in your hands and you need to justify your role as an owner. You need to make sure that you take the necessary steps to make your business a success.

## Financial Responsibility

There are no business partners to share your financial responsibility with and, as an entrepreneur, you must make your peace with it. The simple trick is not to let yourself get overwhelmed when you think about the various aspects of the business. Don't get stressed. If your business idea is good enough, and you can put in all the necessary efforts, then you have nothing to fear.

## There are No Shortcuts

Dropshipping is a unique business model and what might work for one business owner might not work for you. Also, there is no tested secret formula to make it big with dropshipping. It is all about applying the principles of business and maximizing your profits.

There are plenty of people who promise instant wealth and success if you can just follow a "simple system" of theirs. However, the truth is that unless you are planning to rob a bank, you cannot get rich in a jiffy. Most successful entrepreneurs might have started their businesses to get rich, but no one can become successful overnight. Well, think about Facebook. During the years 2004 and 2006, it was an obscure website that was accessible only to university students so that they could network with one another. Well, now we all know where Facebook stands, don't we? It takes hard work to build a company, and it isn't easy. If you want to become successful and earn wealth from your business venture, then you need to be patient and resilient.

## Focus on The Needs of Your Audience

You probably feel that you know your target audience. In today's world, there isn't one giant audience base, and instead, they are excessively segmented. So, you need to take some time to conduct the necessary research to understand the needs of your target audience. Your business won't take off if you don't cater to the needs of your target audience. Regardless of your likes and dislikes, your sole focus must be to satisfy the needs of your customers.

## Ditch It

It is good to believe in your idea firmly. However, when it comes to business, it is equally important to differentiate between what is working and what isn't. If you feel that your plan isn't working, then it is foolhardy to stick to it. Instead, try to change the direction. Try a couple of different ideas and see which of those plans works.

## Ask for Help

As a solopreneur, you are on your own. However, don't take this term too literally. No one is proficient at everything. If you aren't good at an aspect of the business, you can hire external help, and there is no shame in it. It is better to ask for help than to make a costly mistake.

## Don't Worry

As an entrepreneur, your main aim to start a business will be to earn a profit. Being profitable is important. However, you are setting yourself up for failure if you expect to rake in profits from the get-go. It takes a while for a business to break even and, in the meantime, you must be patient. Your business needs a constant influx of funds for its growth. So, don't forget to invest back in your business.

## Scalability

If you want to start a realistic passive income business, then there is one other thing that you need to concentrate on apart from your personality, work ethics, and the actual products, and that's scalability. If you want business growth and want to step away from being hands-on fully, then you need to have a solid team in place and automate the right systems. All the owners of successful passive income businesses know how to manage their time by delegating daily tasks to their team members and they have automated the processes that can help them manage their audience. The difference between a six-figure and a seven-figure business owner is the number of checks they are willing to write.

# Chapter 3: Dropshipping

Dropshipping provides goods by directly delivering products to the customer from the manufacturer. In dropshipping, the store doesn't need to keep products in stock. As soon as the store sells a product, it will procure it from a third-party and will directly ship it to the customer. It is a method of retail fulfillment.

It doesn't take a lot of capital to start a dropshipping business, but there is a lot of work that you need to do before you can make your first sale. It isn't merely about finding the perfect product for dropshipping, but you need to find a good supplier, a fulfillment company, and various other things. In this section, you will learn about setting up a dropshipping business.

## Step One: Find a Niche

The first step is to select a niche. You need to understand that you will not only be competing with other drop shippers but various other retailers too. The well-established retailers certainly have a couple of advantages over drop shippers, but they have a significant disadvantage as well. Retailers like Walmart, Office Depot and Best Buy tend to sell numerous products and it means that they cannot be experts in all the products that they sell. As a drop shipper, you can use their weakness to your advantage. You can focus on a specific product and become an expert. So, what is a niche? A niche refers to a specific set of products. For instance, as a drop shipper, you need to choose a specific niche. Office furniture or office desks are quite vague, and a niche product will be standing desks.

There are numerous products to choose from and it can be quite overwhelming to select one. So, here are a couple of things that you can keep in mind to find a great niche for yourself.

As a drop shipper, you need to understand that the effort it takes to sell a $10 or a $1000 item is the same. The typical margin of a drop shipper is about 20%. For instance, if you sell a $10 item, then you will earn $2 per sale. If you sell a $1000 item, then you'll earn $200 per sale. Keep this in mind when you select a product. The ideal product price point needs to be between $200 and $1000.

Penny-pinchers will look for discounts, refunds, and even return items, whereas the Rockefellers will look for boutique-level service. Both categories of customers will likely eat into your margins. The niche you select needs to resonate with the goldilocks zone. You need to look for customers who are willing to spend their money without expecting extravagant attention. The ideal customer base needs to consist of the upper-middle class section of society. The customer needs to be comfortable with the idea of online shopping. If customers are unfamiliar or are suspicious of online shopping, then you will spend all your time trying to process orders via phone.

Drop shippers don't usually sell name-brand products. It is not possible for a drop shipper to add value to a name-brand product or satisfy the needs of a customer looking for a name brand. For instance, if someone wants to buy a PlayStation, they know that they want a PlayStation. It is unlikely that the customer will search for the "best gaming consoles" on Google. Can you name the best standing desk brands? Probably not. So, for such items, it is likely that you will search on Google for the "best standing desks." A search like this will lead the customer to a dropshipping site. It is better to sell generic products because brand names are already listed on different sites.

You can also opt for all those products with limited local retailers. An ideal customer for a dropshipping business is one who will look for the perfect product instead of concentrating on savings. For instance, if someone has to buy an aquarium and finds about ten different options at the local store. The said person is not happy with the options available, so the person hops online and searches for the best aquariums.

The products that you want to choose for your dropshipping business must be light and durable instead of being heavy and fragile. As a drop shipper, you need to consider the logistics involved in the products you want to list. Shipping is the supplier's responsibility, but you are responsible for the customer service involved. Shipping issues are one of the most common issues you will face in customer service. Isn't it better to handle the customer shipping issues for something sturdy like an outdoor fireplace instead of something fragile like porcelain dolls? Also, avoid all products that require a lot of technical support while setting up.

## Step Two: Identify Your Competition

Now that you have selected a niche, the next step is to check your competition. A niche without any competitors is not a good niche. So, any good niche will have some competition in it. Even if it seems counterintuitive, a niche without any competition is probably a bad sign. For instance, a good restaurant will always have a good crowd and it might even be tough to get a table at times. On the other hand, a deserted restaurant probably implies that the service or the food isn't that good. Well, it might be an undiscovered gem, but chances are that diners don't usually prefer the deserted restaurant and assume that it is deserted for a reason.

If your niche doesn't have any competition, it is likely that other businesses don't seem to think it is profitable. Maybe the niche doesn't have as many customers as you seem to think, probably the suppliers aren't good enough, or maybe the logistics are too high. Regardless of the reason, you must not waste your time on a niche that isn't profitable. If there is competition, it means that people are able to earn a profit and that's exactly what you are trying to do as well.

So, how can you find your competitors? The first thing you need to do is run a Google search on your niche and then select the Shopping tab on Google. Now, click on the products displayed and follow the links. Once you do this, you need to establish if the other sellers are drop shippers or traditional sellers. Remember that your aim is not to compete with traditional retailers. So, you need to find a niche that will help you as a drop shipper.

To establish whether your competitor is a drop shipper or a traditional retailer, you need to check their locations. If they are present in multiple locations, then they are a retailer. After you do this, you need to search for their registered address on Google Maps. If it is an online store, then you will find that it is listed as a Verizon store on Google maps.

## Step Three: Identify the Best Suppliers

As a drop shipper, you will fully rely on suppliers to fulfill the orders you receive. There are some suppliers that are reliable, and they generally have an inventory of their stock and they will ship the products on the desired dates. If you find a supplier like this, then the said supplier is a top tier supplier. On the other hand, the not-so-good suppliers tend to do the exact opposite and it will simply increase your maintenance costs.

Once you identify your niche and your competitors, the next step is to identify your suppliers. You don't have to start contacting suppliers yet, but you need to know the prospects you are trying to impress. By researching your niche, you are now aware of your competitors and their suppliers who are making them money.

Instead of taking a risk by approaching unproven partners, it is a good idea to use this information. It is easy to identify products and brands that are doing well for your competitors. Such products will be listed front and center on their official site to increase their visibility to the customers. They can even be listed under either the most popular or the most popular brand categories/pages.

Now, it is time for you to get working. You need to make a list of all the brands, the product names, and the stock keeping unit numbers according to your niche. You need to repeat this step for all your competitors and make a list of all the brands and products that you see often. This information will come in handy when you are looking for future suppliers.

You might wonder if there is an easier way to make a list of the top-tier sellers in your niche. Well, the suppliers that you are looking for aren't that good at marketing and that's why you need to do a little leg work. So, if you search for something like "Standing desk dropship suppliers", it is unlikely that you will find a dropshipping partner. Google search might also display supplier aggregators.

Aggregators are aware that drop shippers tend to find it difficult to find the right suppliers. So, they sell access to the list of suppliers. For a fledgling drop shipper, it might seem like a viable option to pay for an aggregator to obtain the list of suppliers. Aggregators tend to attract a lot of drop shippers who are merely looking for shortcuts and the top tier suppliers don't usually want to collaborate with someone who takes shortcuts. Top tier suppliers also don't like the idea of wasting their time screening through the list of short-cutters to find a viable dropshipping partner. So, while an aggregator might connect you to a willing supplier, it is possible that those suppliers will never be your business's top partners. There are several popular aggregators like Worldwide Brands, DOBA, and Dropship Direct.

When you start to search your competitor's websites for a list of suppliers, make a note of all the things that you like and don't like about their websites and online stores. You can use all this information when you design a storefront for your dropshipping business. If you want to know the popularity of your competitor's websites, then you can enter their URL into compete.com. You need to pay some attention to the sites that are popular and you can incorporate those features into your own site.

Once you compile a list of all the suppliers of your competitors, the next step is to verify those suppliers. The two criteria they need to meet are MAP policy enforcement and no pay-to-play.

**MAP Policies**

Minimum Advertised Price policies or MAP polices are the set of rules that a supplier has to protect its brand value as well as its retail partners. The lowest price at which a retailer can sell the supplier's product is known as the MAP. You need to work with a supplier who not only has a MAP policy but also make sure that the policy is enforceable. The enforceability of MAP policies is essential because, without it, there will be a price war. A price war is a race to the bottom. As a drop shipper, your profit margins will wear out and the brand value of the suppliers will decrease. A top-tier supplier understands this and will certainly enforce their MAP policies.

You can tell whether a potential supplier enforces their MAP policies or not by simply searching for their product on Google Shopping. You must be able to see various listings of the same product. You are trying to figure out the common lowest price. For instance, if the lowest price of a listed product is $340 and if the product is not listed below this price by the retailers, then it means that the supplier is enforcing the MAP. If some listings of the product are below that price, then the supplier isn't strictly enforcing their MAP policies. For a drop shipper, the MAP also shows the lowest margin available on a product. If the margin is quite lean at MAP, then it is ideal that you look for alternatives with a higher MAP.

**No Pay-To-Play**

Any supplier who makes drop shippers pay a monthly or annual fee to sell their products is certainly not a top-tier supplier. It is an indicator that the supplier is more interested in earning money and not building their brand. A top-tier supplier will always value a dropshipping store since it can introduce their products to interested customers and other potential customers. Usually, you will need to either call or email the supplier to know their pay-to-play policy. Most suppliers usually provide the appropriate contact information for these sorts of enquiries on their site. There is a difference between aggregator fees and the pay-to-play fees of the suppliers.

A couple of other qualities that you need to look for in an ideal seller are:

- Whether the supplier instantly updates you about their inventory levels or not
- A comprehensive listing of their online products
- Order history
- Any customizable data feeds
- A favorable return policy
- Anything else that will help streamline and automate your work to keep your customers happy

**Step Four: Build Your Website**

Before any supplier will agree to partner with you, you will need a storefront. Suppliers need to be able to see that you are a worthy partner who knows how to not only talk the talk but can walk the walk as well. You don't need to be a web design wiz or a tech guru to build a dropshipping website. There are various e-commerce platforms like Oberlo and Shopify that simplify your work. It is easy to start a dropshipping website. In this section, you will learn about the different things that every dropshipping website needs to have.

The first feature that your dropshipping website needs to have is a sample product listing and brand pages. Your suppliers will want to see how their products will be listed in your store. It is easier to convince a supplier to partner with you if they can readily see their products displayed in a professional and prominent manner on your website. It also shows the suppliers that you are ready to start doing business. So, you need to build your pages in a manner that will appeal to your potential suppliers. Also, it is a good idea to include user reviews of your supplier's products and brands.

There are several companies that provide third-party monitoring as a service. A couple of companies that you can use for this purpose are Merchant Safe, TRUSTe, and Trust Guard. All these companies have badges that you can display on your website. These badges indicate to customers that they can trust your business. It might seem like an insignificant add-on, but it is quite important in the world of e-commerce. It will make your customers and your suppliers feel comfortable and safe while transacting with your business.

Ensure that the shipping and the return policies are stated clearly and aren't ambiguous. Customers don't like discouraging return policies or any hidden shipping costs. Not just customers; even suppliers don't like ambiguous return policies since it will be bad for their business. It is a good idea to dedicate a separate page for your business's shipping and return policies.

You must always include an About Us and a Contact Us page on your website. These pages are quite easy to overlook but are critical for any business. As a drop shipper, you cannot forego either of these pages. Your customers need to know who to contact if they have any queries or any issues with their orders. Keep the About Us page brief and tell your business's story in an engaging manner. The Contact Us page needs to be easy to locate and must include a phone number, email address, hours of operation, instant chat (if possible), and a physical address.

**Step Five: Generate Traffic**

Now, you need to figure out how you can generate traffic to your store. You need a detailed plan to generate and direct traffic to your site if you want to be a successful drop shipper. Suppliers will also need to see this blueprint because there is no point in having a wonderful store without any customers. You need to work on developing marketing strategies to achieve this objective. You can generate traffic for your dropshipping site in different ways. The first method is to use Google AdWords. Other methods include Google Product Listing Ads, Facebook Ads, retargeting, email offers, and niche blogs. Once you have a supplier onboard, or if you have a potential supplier, then they will want to know about your plan to generate traffic via marketing and advertising. So, you need to have a dedicated marketing and advertising budget.

**Step Six: Register Your Business**

Before you contact the suppliers to set up any dropshipping deals, you must register your business. You need to form and register your business with the appropriate authorities. Apart from income tax, dropshipping also attracts certain sales tax and sales tax exemptions. Most suppliers require the drop shipper to have an EIN or Employer Identification Number and a Sales Tax Exemption permit before they approve you as a dropshipping partner for their business.

**Step Seven: Secure a Dropship Agreement**

A lot of sellers merely add the supplier's products to their store and it is not good practice. Sellers have to understand that, in order to seem desirable to their supplier, they need to have a sales channel that promises good returns. Suppliers always like sellers who have high-traffic channels like blogs, websites, YouTube channels, and the like.

You need to understand that suppliers will not come knocking at your door. You need to don your sales hat and start working on the phone. You need to reach out to all the suppliers you have on your list. Take some time before you decide to choose a specific seller. Remember that sellers tend to get lots of enquiries and it might take you a couple of tries before they realize that you mean serious business and that they might be a potential partner in your venture. So, you must stay positive and have an effective pitch ready.

Ensure that you contact a lot of suppliers since not many companies might want to drop ship. It is a good idea to talk to them on the phone or even visit them in person to show your willingness to create a working relationship.

You need to set a launch date for your site. The launch date signifies that you are serious about your business proposal and that you want to start selling. A launch date also makes the supplier consider that, if your site doesn't list their products by then, then you will list someone else's products. It is important to have a timeline so that you can get started with your business. It also makes the supplier take you seriously and consider your business prospect seriously.

If all goes well up to this point, the next thing you need to figure out is your terms of payment. A supplier will obviously want to know about your payment options. Usually, drop shippers tend to pay their suppliers either upfront or they pay on terms. If you opt for the former, then you will need to pay the supplier as soon as an order is placed. If you opt for the latter, then you agree to pay the supplier at a later date (usually within 30 days). You need to be upfront and quite clear about your payment terms.

## Dropshipping Tips

### Work on Marketing

There are different aspects of a dropshipping business that you can automate these days. When you automate your business, you will have more time to focus on marketing and branding strategies. Designing the logo, creating the content, creating graphics, and other posts can be quite fun to do, but if you want to start raking in some profits, you need to concentrate on marketing. You need to spend some time learning about how ads work, increase your web traffic, and also work on converting visitors to your online store.

The two best strategies that you can use to increase web traffic to your site are ads and SEO. You need to remember that the conversion rate for most e-Commerce stores is 1-2%. It means that if the number of visitors to your store is less than 100, then you will not be able to earn any profits. The higher the traffic to your store, the greater your chances of conversion. Most drop shippers focus on ads; they might produce instant gratification and help increase sales in a short duration. If you are looking for ways to drive up your sales in the long run, then you need to concentrate on SEO. SEO increases your ranking on search engines and increases your online visibility. You can ensure that your acquisition costs stay low and reach a wider audience with a minimal ad budget if you can create blog content and start optimizing your product pages.

You must also optimize your website for conversions. If you want to compel or tempt people to make a purchase, then don't forget to use scarcity and urgency to increase the chances of sales. To ensure that you are optimizing your business's online website properly, you need to increase the instances of impulsive buying, add some favorable customer reviews as well as testimonials, and do everything you can to make the website look appealing and attractive to your customers.

## Amazing Offer

An extremely important tip of dropshipping is that you need to create a compelling offer. You must not end up like all those storeowners who fail to include sales or bundles. If you notice that none of your store's products are on sale, then visitors might lack the initial motivation necessary to purchase something. If you can manage to present the right product with a good deal, then your rate of conversion will certainly increase.

Another thing that seems to work really well in the world of dropshipping is bundle deals. Whenever you decide to create a bundle deal, you need to focus on selling more items of a specific product. For instance, if you are dropshipping hair extensions, then a bundle will include more hair extensions. If your target audience seems to like the product, then they will certainly want more of it. The tricky bit is to convince your customers to not just make a purchase, but once they decide to purchase something you must upsell it. For instance, if you are ordering something and you see a combo offer on something else that interests you, then it is quite likely that you will want to buy both the items displayed.

## Don't Underprice

There are certain platforms that allow you to maintain a lower product cost. You can make a profit on your sales if the cost of goods is reasonably close to the wholesale price and you can sell your products at market value. The goal of a dropshipping business like any usual business is to earn profits. If you decide to sell a $5 product, then make sure that you are charging $19 and more for it, if you want to be profitable. You must never underprice your products. Always consider different aspects of the business like the cost of the goods, marketing expenses, other business expenses, and any other expenses related to the potential expansion of the business.

Don't undercut your prices merely because other dropshipping businesses are undercutting their prices. You don't have to worry about undercutting your prices as long as they are fair and are within market value. You must try to increase your average order value if you want to earn a higher return from the orders you receive. If you want to earn a higher return, then you need to come up with creative strategies that will help you upsell.

## Quality Suppliers

Most suppliers that you come across are usually reliable, offer good products, and are easy to work with. At times, you might find suppliers who don't offer any of these things. Whenever you are selecting a supplier, make sure that you spend some time to thoroughly vet the supplier. As a drop shipper, the rate of success of your business depends on the quality of suppliers that you find. Make sure that the suppliers you opt to have sufficient staff on hand to ensure prompt delivery of packages. You can use a platform like Oberlo to find a reliable supplier.

## Automate Your Business

If you use any of the dropshipping tools like Oberlo, then several aspects of your business will be automated. If you have a full-time job or you want to generate passive income, then you need to come up with different ways in which you can automate various aspects of your business. If you automate your business, you will have more time to pursue your passions. There are different ecommerce tools that will help to automate, grow, and scale your business. For instance, Buffer lets you automate your social media posts and Kit helps you automate different marketing activities like advertising, retargeting, email marketing, and more. There are different marketing automation software available on the market that will simplify your work for you.

## A Presentable Website

A critical aspect of dropshipping that you cannot afford to ignore is your business website. You need to make sure that the website is customer-friendly and easy to use. The website you create needs to appeal to customers and must not scare them off. A lot of newbie business owners start to market their business even when the home page of their site lacks certain important details like a placeholder text, a well-defined product list, and other important images. Before you decide to launch your store online, you need to take a look at the websites of your competitors in your niche. What does their website look like? What are the things they included on their homepage? Is their website easy to navigate? Do they use their logos or include their logos on their images? What are the types of pages on their website and are the pages optimized to increase conversions?

Once you look at a couple of different websites, you will have a general idea of all the things that you must and must not do. There will be certain aspects of these websites that will impress you, so try to imitate those features. Your dropshipping business's website is as important as the physical façade of a brick and mortar store. You need to make sure that your website appeals to viewers instantly and encourages them to make a purchase.

## Don't Forget about Your Competition

An important business tip is that you must never forget about your competition. This tip applies to dropshipping as well. You must always be updated about the different marketing strategies your competition adopts, their scalability, and such other things. In fact, a simple way in which you can keep track of the way your competitors are doing is by following their profiles on social media. If you do this, you will have the perfect opportunity to track and measure their progress. Also, it might give you some ideas on how to change your own marketing strategy.

You can also gauge the profitability of a certain product, its demand, and popularity amongst users. When you start paying attention to these details, your business will certainly do well.

**Trustworthy Brand**

You need to take up the responsibility for the functioning of your brand and you are the only one that's responsible for the way you represent it. If you strengthen the positioning of your brand, you can strengthen your reputation as a leader as well. Look at the different things that make your business unique. Think about the various aspects of the business that you can leverage to strengthen your brand's image. You need to concentrate on building trust by building your brand's image and increasing brand awareness amongst your target audience. Your brand is a mere extension of your business's personality. A strong brand image will certainly assist in increasing your business's value and will make it more memorable for your customers.

## Chapter 4: Amazon FBA

Fulfillment by Amazon is popularly known as FBA and is a third-party logistics service started by Amazon. It helps millions of sellers registered with Amazon all across the globe fulfill their orders. FBA provides you with the option of shipping your old as well as new products to Amazon, instead of shipping them directly to your customers. Once your products reach the Amazon Fulfillment Centers, they will handle the rest. As and when orders are placed for your products, Amazon will directly pick the stock up from these fulfillment centers and ship them to customers. They will provide you with shipping facilities, customer service once the order is delivered, and manage customer returns. It will help you save a significant amount of time, effort, and money. Many sellers who have opted for FBA have ended up saving approximately 50% on shipping costs.

The working of FBA can be summed up in one sentence: "you sell it, we ship it." A private label seller must make the most of Amazon's fulfillment network and their expertise to help in the growth of their business. Your listings on Amazon.com can make use of the free shipping services offered by Amazon, provided the bill amount is above a specified value.

The FBA listings on Amazon.com are listed and then sorted according to price, and there are no shipping costs involved if the combined value of products is above the amount of $35. The FBA listings, when accompanied by the FBA logo, let customers know that the shipping, packing, customer service, and all returns are handled solely by Amazon. Fulfillment of orders even from other sales channels can be completed by using the inventory stored at the Amazon fulfillment center. The online user interface will let you manage your list and at the same time will provide the necessary direction so that the inventory can be returned at any time.

The following steps explain in brief how the process of FBA works:

**Sending of Products to Amazon**

You can send your products, new and used, to Amazon's fulfillment center. Seller Central uploads the details of your listings. You can decide whether you want Amazon to fulfill either partly or in whole of your inventory or not. You can use FBA's Label Service to print labels, or you can also make use of PDF Labels, which are provided by Amazon. Either you can select your carrier, or you can make use of Amazon's discounted shipping facility.

As soon as the products are received by Amazon, it scans the inventory. The unit dimensions for storage are recorded. Your list can be monitored by using Amazon's integrated tracking system. The products received are cataloged and stored.

The orders placed are fulfilled by Amazon regardless of whether it has been put on Amazon.com or any other fulfillment request has been sent to sales, not on Amazon.

Web-to-warehouse, sorting system and high-speed picking system, are the technologies adopted by Amazon that let it locate the desired outcomes. Customers have the option of combining products.

The products are shipped to customers through Amazon's fulfillment centers. The products are shipped to the customer depending upon the method selected by them. The required tracking information of the products dispatched is sent to the customer. Customer service can always be contacted for orders placed on Amazon.com.

Here are some simple steps that you can follow for adding Fulfillment by Amazon to your selling on Amazon Account:

Go to the Inventory option and click on Manage Inventory.

For selecting a product that you want to include in the FBA listing, just click on the box next to it in the left column

Now go to Actions and click on Changed to Fulfilled by Amazon.

And then, all you need to do is follow the directions given to create your first shipment.

**Things Needed**

A Smartphone: A Smartphone is a multidisciplinary tool that finds use in almost all sectors. In the modern age, this device has proved to be a necessity rather than a luxury. A computer with an active Internet connection is also useful. As your business develops, a Smartphone will be preferred as it gives you a greater sense of flexibility.

A scouting app: A scouting app is handy for a developing business, which can be easily installed on your Smartphone.

A printer: A good quality inkjet color printer with A4 paper sheets (11×17 inches long grain paper).

Packaging equipment: This is the main component of the toolkit. As a seller, you must never run out of these tools. Stack up on your cartons, boxes, labeling sheets, tapes, and other stationery that you use for packaging your products.

**How to Use FBA**

FBA stands for Fulfillment by Amazon. In this section, you will learn about the complete process of selling on Amazon. Follow these simple steps, and you can start to sell items using FBA:

**Step 1: Create a Seller Account**

The first thing you need to do is create a seller account on Amazon. If you have one, that's good, if you don't then create one for yourself. The first thing you need to choose is a Professional or an Individual account. The answer to this is simple. If you plan to sell more than 40 items a month, then you must opt for the Professional account, if not you can use an Individual account. Amazon has a 40-items cutoff. When you use an Individual account to sell, Amazon will charge you $1 per item. If you plan to sell 40 items in a month, then you might as well pay the $40 to create a Professional account. Once you select the account type, you have to login or create an Amazon account with your choice of email. After that, you will need to provide information about the method of charge, seller information, and provide identity verification. You must opt for a credit card as your charge method. It will not be charged automatically, so you needn't worry.

When you fill out the seller information, you must give your name, address, and create a Display name for yourself. The "Display name" is the name that buyers will see next to your listing of items. It can be anything that you want, but remember that it is a public name. Select a suitable display name, and it must not sound shady. You can verify your identity via a phone call or a text message. And voila! You have successfully created your seller account.

## Step 2: List the Items

Once you set up your seller account, the next step is to list all the items that you wish to sell. If you aren't sure about the items that you can sell, you can start with some items you find around your home. Once you figure out the items you want to sell, you need to list them on your seller account. To add a product, you must go to the Inventory option at the top of your screen and click on the "Add Product" option. Once you select this option, you can search for the product with the help of the barcode or the product name. Unless you sell something that you manufactured by yourself, you don't have to create a new product. You can sell anything that you want. Once you select the product, you must add the product information. You need to mention the selling price of the item, the condition of the item, and whether you will ship the product yourself or whether Amazon will ship it for you. For pricing, you can enter an amount that you feel comfortable with. To price your items, you can go through the price list of similar items and fix a price accordingly. When you describe the condition of the items, try to be as descriptive as you can and be honest too. Select any of the options like "acceptable," "good," "new," or anything else accordingly. However, it is better if you offer an additional description. Be honest about the condition that the item is in and don't exaggerate. You don't want the customer to return your item or ask for a refund, do you? So, be honest if you're going to avoid negative reviews. Since you want to use the FBA option, you must select the same for the shipping method. If you are using FBA for the first time, then Amazon will provide you with a registration screen with the terms and conditions that are applicable. Go through this page carefully and accept the terms if you agree.

## Step 3: Convert Your Items

You need to convert your items to FBA items. You might wonder why you must do this if you selected the FBA option in the previous step. Well, the answer is quite simple. Amazon has specific policies and to use their FBA service you need to convert your items to Fulfillment by Amazon items. To convert your items, you must go to your inventory, select the *"manage inventory"* option. You will find a drop-down list of *"actions"* and select the *"Change to Fulfilled by Amazon"* option. Once you select this option, you will find two preferences. The two options available are *'FBA Label Service'* and *'Sticker-less Commingled Inventory'*. If you want to sell a new item, then you can use the second option.

In this, Amazon will mix your units with those of other sellers who sell similar items. If someone places an order for a similar item like yours, then Amazon may ship the buyer a unit from either your stock or some other seller. The FBA Label Service is quite important. It allows Amazon to place a label on your items and you don't have to do it yourself. If you don't want to print your labels, then this is the best option for you. It costs about 20 cents per item if you avail of this service. If you want to increase your profit margin, then you can label the products by yourself. Once you select either of the options, you will be given two choices by Amazon. The first option is "Convert Only" and the second option is "Convert and Send Inventory." If you select the convert only, then you can add more items to your inventory before you ship it to the Amazon warehouse. After you complete all these steps, you will notice that your items will appear under the heading of "Amazon-Fulfilled Inventory."

**Step 4: Shipping Plan**

If you select the "Convert and Send Inventory" option, or if you have just added another option, the next step is to create a shipping plan for the items. You need to list the "Ship from" address and the packing you require. The two types of packing available are individual items and case-packed items. The choice depends on the kind of product or item you want to sell. Once you create your shipping plan, the next step is to add the items. I am assuming that this is the second item that you added so that you will see two items. Now you must select both the items or as many items as you wish to sell. You must repeat the same process for all items you want to add, and, in the end, you must select the "add to an existing shipping plan" option instead of a "create a new shipping plan" option.

## Step 5: Ship Your Products

Now that you have listed all the items, you must ship them. To send your products or units, you need to go to the inventory, click on the *"Manage FBA shipments"* and click on the *"Continue with shipping plan."* Enter the number of items that you want to ship. If your items require any prep, select whether you want Amazon to do the prep or not. Lastly, you must choose if you or Amazon can label the product. When the products are ready to be shipped, weigh them once. Print the labels and stick them on the package. After this, they are prepared to be sent and drop them off at a local UPS.

## Step 6: Sell Your First Item

It is the most straightforward step of all. Once you ship the package to Amazon and they receive it, your items are now officially available for purchase. Now, all that you need to do is wait for a buyer to make a purchase. If the product you decide to sell is one of the popular ones, then you will be able to sell it within a week or two.

By now you will have sold a product. If not, at least your products are now available on Amazon.

# Chapter 5: Email List and Email Follow Up

If you want to successfully market your business, then you need to have an engaged email list. You might have something valuable to offer your potential customers, but how can you make them give you their email address? Fortunately, there are a couple of different ways in which you can grow your email subscriber list. In this section, you will learn about all these methods.

## A Sign-Up Button

It isn't necessary that everyone who reads your emails is on your email list. For instance, if you share your email address on social media, it's not necessary that all your followers will be on your email list. People might also forward your email to their friends. If you know that you put some valuable content in the email, then people will share it. So, whenever you send out a new newsletter, you can get subscribers. To make it easy for visitors to sign up, you can add a join my email list link to any of the emails you send.

## Sign-Up Form on Your Website

Your website will be the first contact for a lot of people who want to do business with you. You must not miss this opportunity to connect with new visitors. You can include a sign-up form on your website so that all those who are interested can sign up immediately.

## At Events

If you host any events where people can register or where they need to purchase tickets for in advance, then you can even collect contact information at such events. In fact, it is the perfect time to encourage people to subscribe to your email list. When you collect information from registrants, it gives you an opportunity to communicate with the attendees.

## Industry Tradeshows

Industry events, conferences, or even tradeshows are a great place to increase your email list. Such events provide you with the opportunity to connect with new customers as well as similar businesses. You can put up a sign-up list at the conference and even on your website.

## Existing Database

Never overlook your existing database of contacts that you have with you. It can include your colleagues, acquaintances, friends, or even family members. It is a good place to start growing your email list. Initially, your email list might just include your friends and family members, but after a while, it will grow. Take the feedback that you receive from your existing contacts and make the necessary changes to move ahead. You can even make them spread the word about your business.

## Downloadable Whitepaper

You can use a couple of lead magnets to grow your email list. A simple way in which you can grow your customer relationships is to offer them a lead magnet like a whitepaper or any other educational resource in exchange for their email address. Ensure that the content you offer is unique, resourceful, and entertaining. It must engage and encourage your audience to subscribe to your list. Or perhaps you can offer a glimpse at a whitepaper or any other educational resource and provide the rest to the reader once they sign up. It is a simple way to gather new leads.

### Sign-Up with Their Phone

You need to make it convenient for your existing and potential customers to join your email list by enabling them to sign-up using their phones. For instance, the Text-to-Join tool of Constant Contact enables people to join your email list by sending a text message along with a code that is unique to your business.

### Membership Forms

If you have plans of offering membership, then you can include a sign-up option on such forms. It will encourage people to sign up and it will not even look like you are trying hard to grow your email list.

### Social Media

You can include a sign-up page on your business's Facebook page. Social media is a wonderful tool that you can use to increase your reach. You can encourage and prompt your followers and fans to subscribe to your mailing list by including a simple sign-up form on your Facebook page. You can even include a sign-up form on your Instagram page as well. The one thing that you need to ensure for this technique to work is that you post exceptional and engaging content on your profiles. If your profile impresses the viewer, then it is quite likely that they will be willing to sign up for your email list as well.

### Facebook Ads

You can run a Facebook ad to increase your business's reach. You can use Facebook ads to grow your email list. Instead of using a Facebook ad to drive traffic to your page, you can run an ad to encourage people to sign-up for your email list.

**Exclusive Access**

Exclusivity is the best way to grow your email list. If you can offer something that will interest your audience, that they will not find anywhere else, then it will encourage them to sign-up for your email list. So, you need to be able to create useful and interesting content that is unique to your email list.

Now that you are aware of the different techniques that you can follow to grow your email list, the next step is to implement these tips.

# Chapter 6: Sales Funnels

A sales funnel is the path that enables a potential customer to move from the stage of awareness of the product to interest, desire, and finally to make a purchase. It is important that you create a sales funnel for your business. It might seem like a small aspect of a business, but it has the potential to increase your sales. A sales funnel is like a business plan that leads a prospect from their "I don't know" phase to the "let us do business" stage. A sale doesn't happen, and at times, the potential customer needs a little encouragement to go ahead and make the purchase. In this section, you will learn about the different steps that you can follow to create a sales funnel for your business.

## Identify Your Prospects

Before you can devise a plan to encourage a potential prospect to do business with you, the first thing you need to do is identify your prospects. Your goal is to direct the interested parties from the wide end to the narrow end of the funnel. So, the first thing that you need to do is determine who your ideal customer will be. You can create a questionnaire to help you move along. For instance, if you want to dropship standing desks, then who will be your target audience? Is it just for businesses or even private individuals? What is the demographic of your target audience? Who will the product appeal to? Ask yourself a couple of simple questions and you will have an idea of your target audience.

## Qualify Your Prospects

A person might fit into your profile of an ideal customer, but it doesn't mean that such a person is necessarily an ideal customer. Maybe someone has a business, but they don't like standing desks, then such a business might fit all your requirements of an ideal customer but their lack of desire for the product you offer disqualifies them. So, you need to spend some time and qualify your prospects after identifying them. It is quite simple to qualify prospects. You can conduct a survey or a poll; you can even talk to people about their needs or you can create a product that you know will appeal to your target audience. Without the right audience, you cannot increase your sales even if you have a wonderful product.

## Apply the Fundamentals

Your sales funnel is a means to direct your prospects as well as potential customers to your business to finalize a sale. For instance, if you have a blog that you post daily, you can promote the blog on social media to increase the customer's attention to your business. Once your prospects land on your blog, you can encourage them with an offer to obtain their email address. You can then start to send out emails regularly to encourage those prospects to make a purchase. One thing that you can do is start by selling something that is easily affordable to your prospects like a $20 item. Once they make a purchase, you will have a list of confirmed buyers. Once you have this list, you can start to send them a list of higher-priced products to drive the prospects deeper into the sales funnel.

## Establish the Sales Funnel

The best way in which you can plan your sales funnel is to start backwards. So, if you have a $200 product, then you will need to find those people who are willing to spend that kind of money for the benefits the product offers. People will spend money on a product you offer, only if they trust you. So, you need to slowly build some trust. A backward plan for a sales process will start with an expensive product, a mid-range product, an introductory product, a free informational piece or a sample, an email sign-up campaign, blog conversation, and social media interaction.

The key is to understand the needs of your customers and to meet those needs.

# Chapter 7: Blogging

Words are said to be more powerful than swords and bullets. Words, when employed cleverly, can win you not just money but also wars and countries. Such is the power of words alone that they are said to be one of the most influential factors in any transaction. Why must your business be deprived of the blessing of words?

Start a blog about your business. A business blog is usually a place where you not only advertise your products and services but also attract customers via the same. A blog can provide all or any of the following kinds of information:
The description of the exact products and services your online business has got to offer. This blog can use the power of creativity to make sure that not only are your customers informed but attracted as well.

Know the pros and cons of a particular product or service. Your blog is supposed to be a platform where the general public gets to know about the unbiased opinions about your business. Do not always praise and boast about your successes. Admit defeats by warning your customers against some slip-ups you might have made.

## Guidance

The best form of help you can provide via a blog is guiding your clients regarding any queries they might have about a product or a service. Open a hotline number that is to be managed by an employee the entire day. Any aggrieved or curious person can contact this number in case they've got a complaint or are simply curious.

**Reviews**

Invite people to give reviews about your business. If you have worked decently so far and your business has been in the market for a fair amount of time, people are bound to have liked your service. Why refrain from exploiting their satisfaction to further gain in the popularity sector? Allow people to leave star ratings and good feedback by including a box for feedback on your website.

Your blog need not necessarily be about your business alone. It can be about the general market as well. You can review other businesses and the entire market if you have the time, thereby establishing a good platform for customers to come and get honest views not just from consumers but also from an established business person, which is you.

Blogging is a great way to make sure that your business reaches out to people and because everything is online, you do not have to sweat it out in the sun hanging posters and running for billboard authorities. Hire a good web designer who can set up a well-maintained website for you to operate.

Make sure you are well acquainted with the functions of all the features of the blog and your website. Do not write just for the sake of it; write so as to keep the average customer informed and entertained. Your graph keeps going up as long as you are regular with your blog. When you are irregular, people lose interest after a while, and that affects your credibility as a businessman since they cannot trust you to deliver on time and at a uniform frequency. Moreover, they also lose out on getting updated with the recent developments in the product or service they have subscribed to or bought from you. These days anyone who has an internet connection has got a blog of his own and does not require any official publication to let people know his or her views on things, ranging from life issues to scientific ones. Starting a blog is a great booster to your online venture.

**Search Engine Optimization**

Have you ever tried to look up a specific thing on Google? If yes, then you must be aware of how Google shows you results, yes? Say if you typed in the search bar ''Tiger'', it will show you all possible results related, remotely or otherwise, to the animal tiger. However, if there has recently been a warship named 'Tiger,' and the same has caused ripples in the social media world, then this piece of news is going to appear before any other. Have you ever thought as to why the results are arranged the way are? The answer is Search Engine Optimization.

The idea is very simple. When you write about your products or services, you have to be as simple as a worker bee. You cannot afford to clutter your blogs with content that has very little to do with what the core of your business is or is supposed to be. Be precise when talking about your product. If you have an associated website to your online business, make sure its content does not beat around the bush and does not contain matter that is irrelevant to the fundamental principles of your business. Search Engine Optimization is a great way to regulate, which search appears first and which one appears last when an innocent consumer decides to find out about your merits on the Internet.

Blogging is quite a trendy activity these days. A blog will help increase the reach of your business in the marketplace. Your business is a powerful system that can satisfy the needs of a target audience. Before your products can satisfy anyone's wants or needs, you need to supply your business with a constant flow of interested customers. So, how do you do this? You can do this by running a blog. A blog will help direct traffic to your business's site as well.

What are the benefits of blogging? Blogging will help direct more traffic to your business's site through SEO. You can include call-to-actions or CTAs in your blog posts to generate new leads for your business. If you share quality and engaging content, then it will improve your authority in the concerned field. It is also a great means to connect with your audience. Apart from all this, it also acts as a feedback machinery to receive feedback from all those who visit your blog. Here are the steps that you can follow to start blogging:

## Create Content

The first step is to create good content for your blog. If you use a free service to host your blog, then you can go through the tutorial it offers to go through the initial stages of setting up a blog. If you host your site, then you need a little experience with web design to customize your blog. Content is king, and you need to have compelling content if you want to earn money from your blog. You must come up with new and innovative topics to write about. If not a new topic, then you must offer some fresh perspective on existing subjects. Learn to present information compellingly. The writing style of your blog must be easy to understand and enjoyable for the reader. If you have a flair for writing, then this is the perfect outlet for your creativity. You need to post regularly, and you must update your blog frequently. If you promise to post one post every alternate day, then make sure that you stick to your promise.

## Use Social Media

Social media is a powerful tool. Where is your target audience these days? How do they spend their time and how can you find them? How can you attract your target audience to your business? Well, social media channels are the answer to all these questions. Almost everyone is active on one social media platform or the other these days. So, you need to share valuable content with your target audience on social media.

**Guest Posts**

If you want to increase your blog's reach, then you can contribute to other blogs present in your niche with relevant content that will interest your audience. You need to comprise a list of blogs that you can approach with your proposal. You can write free guest posts for these blogs in return for a backlink to your business site or your own blog. The growth of your blog is directly proportional to the growth of your business.

**Feedback**

You can use your blog to obtain feedback from your customers and interact with them. After all, all those who regularly follow your blog have mostly purchased something from your site. At the end of the blog post, you can encourage your readers to share their opinions and give their feedback. You can work on the feedback you receive. If you receive any positive feedback, it will encourage other readers to make a purchase. Negative feedback, on the other hand, will help you identify the areas of your business that you need to improve.

**Marketing Your Blog**

Now that you have a blog, the next step is to market your blog. You cannot gain new readers if you do not promote and market your blog. When it comes to promoting your blog, you can start with a couple of keywords for every post.

Keywords are quite relevant, and they help with the SEO ranking of your blog posts. So, every post that you write ensures that you select a couple of keywords that people tend to use frequently to increase the visibility of your work. Not just that, it will also help to improve your audience. There are different keyword research tools that you can use, like Google Keyword Research. Once you find a couple of keywords that you can associate with your blog posts, you need to include them in critical places. The important places to add keywords are the titles of posts, headers, and even in a couple of sentences on your blog. Change the settings on the platform such that the URL of your blog posts include the title and not the date on which it was posted. The title of your blog posts must be descriptive yet brief.

Social media has become an integral part of today's world. Whenever you post something new on your blog, make sure that you post links to your blog on different social media platforms. The idea is to increase traffic to your blog as much as you possibly can. To increase blog traffic, you need a larger audience.

What can be better than social media to find a broader audience? You need to be active on blogging platforms and start to follow other related blogs as well. Paid adverts are an excellent way to market your blog. However, it is better if you can gain natural leads instead of artificially generated leads. Try to use ads on Facebook, StumbleUpon, or even Google AdSense.

## Chapter 8: Market Research and Niche Products

If you want to become a successful seller, then you must think about niche marketing and selling. You must consider starting your niche store. A niche is a small part or the sub-market of a broader market. Niche stores are usually very competitive, and they have the right demand for the product they are selling.

### Find a Niche

You will need to find a niche that suits you and the requirements you have in mind. When you do find a niche that you like, type the same into the search bar provided on eBay. It will help you to check out the competition that exists. Since you are just getting started with niche selling, make sure that there isn't too much competition. If not, you will have a tough time selling. Look into different sub-categories of niches as well. Even if it sounds eccentric, it might be lucrative. Do a lot of research and don't just stick to the most obvious options that are available online.

### Select a Product

You will need to select a product that you want to sell! eBay and Shopify have numerous sellers listed on it. Opening up your niche shop is an excellent idea if you were always interested in starting your own business.

### Your Competition

Make it difficult for your competition to offer the same products that you are offering. Or make your pricing strategy attractive. You must have a unique selling point or USP that will differentiate you from all the other sellers within your niche. Also, make sure that the market is large enough for you to survive.

**Setting up Your Store**

There are some ways in which you can personalize your storefront. This personalization is of great importance to ensure that your store stands apart from the rest; you can quickly grab the attention of potential customers, and promote your brand. You can add a banner to your storefront. A banner is a graphic that will run across the page of your store, and you can create this without much difficulty by making use of graphics software and programs like Picasa, Photoshop, Windows Paint and so on. Always include a shop title and shop announcement. Your shop title will be similar to a tagline, and it will sum up in brief what your shop is all about. Shop announcement is different from a shop title; this will be appearing on the banner, providing information about the products you sell, the materials used, and your artistic philosophy, if any exists.

Your shop announcement can also be made use of for broadcasting about any upcoming events. There are different types of items that you might sell. If you are selling products like notebooks, magnets, pens, picture frames, then you can organize this as stationery, and you can make use of further sections like size, type, material, or price.

When you start selling your products or goods in your eBay or Shopify store, you might wonder about the amount you must charge customers for your items. If you want to have a profitable online shop on these platforms, then you will need to be comfortable going over some numbers and doing a little math regarding your pricing strategy. There are two simple formulae that you will need to learn about this, and they aren't difficult.

The first one is:

(Materials+Labor+Overhead) x2 = Wholesale price

And the second one is:

Wholesale price x2 = Retail price.

But the cost of shipping isn't included in this. The second formula can be adjusted according to your convenience. When you multiply the wholesale price by 2, it will provide the retail price. At times, sellers opt for a number higher than two like 2.5 or 3 for determining their retail price, provided that the market is willing to bear such an expense.

Product photos that are well photographed can act as a catalyst for promoting sales for your eBay store, but you needn't hire a professional photographer to do this. You can very well compose your photos; here are some pointers that will help you portray your product in the best possible manner. All you need is a little bit of artistic flair, some patience, and the following guidelines. You must angle your camera; this means tilting the camera a little so that it will put the subject matter slightly off center and create some movement and flow. It will produce a picture that is more intriguing. Make sure that you fill the frame with your product so that it not only seems more appealing, but potential buyers can also see how well-crafted your product is. For highlighting your piece dramatically and adding a little bit of panache to it, you can blur the background so that the focus automatically shifts to your product. Always frame your picture with a darker element. You can group your products, especially if you are into designing or creating itsy bitsy products, then for attracting attention, you can arrange several products together so that the buyer can see how cohesive your products are together. Make use of the rule of thirds. It is a straightforward rule; you will need to divide the scene that you are photographing into nine parts by making use of two horizontal and vertical lines like a tic tac toe grid. It will help in piquing the interest of the viewer.

An item title is like a good headline for a product, and it needs to be designed in such a manner that it will grab the buyer's attention and get them to want to read more about that particular item. You will need to keep it short and contain it within 155 characters inclusive of spaces. Describe things at the beginning of the item title so that it will help in improving the chances of searching for a specific item.

# Chapter 9: Customer Service

You need to ensure customer satisfaction if you want your business to grow. Customer service doesn't start after a sale, but it goes on even before a customer makes a purchase. It takes some extra resources, a little time, and money to deliver good customer service. All this extra effort certainly goes a long way in enhancing your customer's overall experience with your business. There is no other form of publicity that works better than the good old word-of-mouth publicity. A happy customer will not only be a repeat customer but will also recommend your business to others. In this section, you will learn about the different aspects of providing good customer service.

## Respect

The first thing you need to do is always treat your customers with respect. Treat customers with respect regardless of their attitude towards your business. After all, customers are essentially the heart of any business. Irate customers can be quite troublesome to deal with, but you need to deal with them patiently and calmly. In fact, an irate customer might also become one of your most loyal customers.

## Feedback

Feedback, regardless of it being positive or negative, is quite important to your business. You need to follow up on any feedback you receive. If it is a positive one, reply to it promptly with a thank you. If it is negative feedback, make sure that you follow it up with a solution and take the necessary action. Feedback is a great opportunity to display your customer service skills and increase the level of customer satisfaction.

## After Sales

Your work doesn't end once you make a sale. You need to make sure that you inform the customer that their support was invaluable to your business. You need to thank them for doing business with you and this is the opportunity to create a touch point. You can use this opportunity to introduce your customers to other products listed on your business website.

Complaints are part and parcel of any business. You need to deal with them in an effective and positive manner. Ensure that you listen to your customer's complaints, apologize for any trouble it caused them, and offer them an appropriate solution. You must not blame the customer. Think of it as an opportunity to make improvements to your business.

## Returns

You need to create a standard procedure to deal with customer returns. If a customer receives a defective product and wants to return it, there needs to be a procedure they can follow. You must be able to replace the defective product within the stipulated time according to your terms of service.

## Customer's Needs and Wants

You need to understand the specific needs and wants of your customers. To do this, you need to reach out to them. If you know what your customer wants, you can offer better service.

## Empathy

Empathy is the ability to understand what others feel. You need to empathize with your customers. Whenever you empathize with your customers, it will create a bond between the two and will make your customers feel welcome.

## Listen

You must understand that a customer is reaching out to you because he or she wants to be heard. So, you need to listen and understand their issue, empathize with them, and address the issue. It means that you must always read their messages thoroughly and understand what they are trying to say.

## Rapport

You need to build a rapport with your customers if you want them to stick around. It means that you can highlight your shared interests and passions to make your business seem friendly to customers. A happy customer is an invaluable asset to any business.

## Employees and Staff

If you have employees and staff working along and for you, then you need to value them. They are your first customer and you need to treat them well to make sure that they are happy. If they are happy, they will serve your customers well. The attitude of employees dictates their interactions with customers.

## Customer Service Standards

You need to set certain service standards. It isn't just about drawing up the standards, but it is also important that your staff comprehends them. Draw up a written document dictating the way customer's expectations need to be handled and can help your business.

These standards will also help gauge the way your employees are dealing with customers. There are different training programs you can use to train your employees to deal with customers. An excellent staff is important for the growth of any business.

**Customer Expectations**

You need to clearly let your customers know all that you can and cannot do. Once you make this clear, it will help customers establish certain expectations. Ensure that your standards as well as policies are clearly mentioned in the descriptions of all the items that you sell.

**FAQ or Help Page**

You need to create a FAQ page or a Help page on your website. These pages will answer the immediate questions that a customer might have. There are so many instances when customers get confused about shipping, billing, and delivery policies. Ensure that you have a reply to all these topics on the FAQ page. You need to make sure that you include contact information on the help page.

Customers need to know who to approach in case of any troubles they face. It is important that you concentrate on providing good customer service. Follow the simple tips given in this chapter to improve your customer service and relations.

# Chapter 10: Branding

So far, you have been working on building the foundation of your business. Give yourself a pat on the back for coming a long way. Without a unique identity, a business is not complete. Branding helps carve an identity for your business. Branding lends personality to your business. For instance, think about your favorite company for a moment. You probably are familiar with their logo, their advertisements, and maybe the slogans they use. These are all important elements of branding. You need to make your business memorable and that's the only way in which you can separate your business from your competitors.

A brand is a company's identity. No two individuals are alike and, similarly, no two businesses are alike, and the brand helps make this differentiation. A brand is your business's personality. A lot of businesses seem to think of branding as a mere afterthought. If your business doesn't have a brand, then it will not be memorable to your customers. A lot of fledgling drop shippers give up and quit because of this. The reason is that they don't spend enough time on branding. There are two aspects of branding and they are internal branding and external branding.

## 1. Internal Branding

Regardless of whether you are a solopreneur or if you have a small team of staff, your business needs internal branding. It might seem like a small aspect, but don't ignore it. Internal branding helps you understand what your business stands for. It is a means of saying that the business focuses on its customers. Your customers cannot see internal branding, but the public presence of your business will reflect the internal attitude of your business. Internal branding helps facilitate optimal work environment and ethics. The mission statements along with the list of values are the two ways to implement internal branding.

Mission statements describe the primary objective of your business. The mission statement of Nordstrom is "to give customers the most compelling shopping experience possible" and that of JetBlue is "to inspire humanity – both in the air and on the ground." A mission statement isn't a business cliché, but it can help stir up some good PR. Mission statements will guide all those involved in your business in all aspects of work. It can improve your morale, establish a positive work environment, and improves communication as well. Take a look at the above-mentioned mission statements; they are all about what the company can do for customers. If you make the mission statement all about your business, then it will not work. Not a lot of drop shippers take the mission statement seriously.

You might not realize it, but a lot of companies work according to their mission statement. For instance, IKEA's primary goal to help people create a better everyday life influences everything they do, from their product design to the store layout. This is the sort of internal structure that you must strive to create for your dropshipping business. It is important that you establish internal branding before you think about working on external branding. Internal branding is like the foundation of construction, and without a foundation, you cannot erect a façade. While drafting the mission statement, there are a couple of things that you must keep in mind.

The mission statement must not be self-serving. You need to put your customer first and don't go overboard using "we" in the statement. Don't get caught up in your ambition and lose track of the customers you need to cater to. Always think about the verbs you can use in the mission statement. You need to include the verb and the recipient in the mission statement. Most mission statements start with "To __." You need to include some verb like inspire, give, or offer and add your intended recipient (customers) in it as well. Think about the reasons why your business does what it does. Every business needs a fundamental reason for its existence. Think about the purpose of your business and include it in your mission statement.

You can make a rough draft of all the possible mission statements and the one statement that best summarizes your goals is your answer. You might also have to change your mission statement as your business grows. Your mission statement must always be in sync with your business objectives and aims.

## 2. External Branding

External branding includes various things like your logo, customer support emails, and your social media presence. Your logo and your business website are amongst the first things that a customer will see. So, it is paramount that you make a good impression. Next, you need to concentrate on the style and tone of the content you use. Text and media are a means of communicating with your customers and you need to ensure that all these aspects are in sync with your business objective. In this section, you will learn about the different elements of external branding.

### Logo Design

There is a reason why companies shell out a lot of their money on logo design. A logo is not a mere design, but it is a way in which people can instantly recognize your business. Take a moment to think about all the logos that are committed to your memory. Human beings are visual creatures, and if you see a logo that you love, it will be committed to your memory. You can use the logo for your social media accounts, on business cards, your email profile, and even for your storefront. The first thing that the customer will see is your business logo, so you need to make it as good as it possibly can be. A good logo might be slightly expensive and that's why a lot of entrepreneurs tend to opt for a logo that they can make it themselves. Unless you are a qualified designer, it is a good idea to hire someone to design your logo.

**Website**

If you want to use a website of your own for dropshipping, then you need to concentrate on your website design. Your website is similar to the storefront of a brick and mortar store. Your website reflects your business. So, you need a website that will give your business a prominent web presence. You know that website design is important, but how many of the websites that you visited in the past week do you remember? You probably don't remember many and that's because an average website doesn't give website design the credit it deserves. Try to avoid a generic look for your site. Your website needs to attract customers and must not kill your rate of conversion. The website needs to appeal to your target audience and it needs to further your business goals.

Whenever you are designing your website, you need to make sure that you are integrating your branding into the site. Your website is a mere extension of your business. So, the theme, fonts, colors, and the images that you use on the website need to be consistent with your brand. The website design needs to be memorable and must be unique. You can either build the site yourself or hire someone to do it for you.

**Content**

Once you have figured out the other aspects of external branding, you need to concentrate on your content. You need to make sure that a fancy website with boring content will not be memorable. You need content for your ads, marketing content, social media posts, product descriptions, and anything else like blog posts or videos and the like. You need to create exceptional content that is consistent with your branding. Good content always helps with conversions. So, you need to make sure that you provide unique, valuable, and interesting content for your audience.

## Chapter 11: Print on Demand

Physical products like t-shirts make a great product. You can use the services of a fulfillment company to handle the time-consuming parts of the business such as printing, order fulfillment, and even shipping. Most print-fulfillment companies don't have a high start-up cost, and you don't need much inventory either. You can also have your products dropshipped. Yes, dropshipping comes in handy in this business. You can sell products and have the same delivered to your customers directly from the manufacturer. Passive income from physical products takes some time and effort. In this section, you will learn about how you can create a t-shirt printing business for yourself sans inventory. That does sound amazing, doesn't it?

### Step 1: Storefront

You might have brilliant designs for t-shirts, but your designs will need a home too. There are multiple commerce solutions to create a virtual storefront for yourself. A couple of things that you must consider while you select a platform for yourself are the monthly costs involved, transaction fees, accessibility, options to customize, and its ability to be integrated with other platforms like email services and social media. Shopify is amongst the best platforms available today. You can quickly create a virtual storefront for yourself. You can have a brand name, design a logo for the brand, and customize your storefront as much as you want.

### Step 2: Print Fulfillment Company

There are different fulfillment companies for you to choose from. You can try

Printful or something like Print Aura or Scalable Press. They offer different styles of t-shirts to choose from and can be easily integrated with other e-commerce platforms. Check their terms and conditions, fees chargeable, and other policies. After all, the print fulfillment company will do most of your work for you. So, you need to make sure that you select the right provider.

## Step 3: Connect the Storefront to the Fulfillment Company

Now that you have an e-commerce platform for your storefront and a print company to fulfill your orders, the next step is to integrate these two. You must not skip this step, or else your requests will not be sent for printing and delivery. You can configure the settings for shipping costs, the shipping address, a customer service email address (other contact information), and invoices too.

## Step 4: Customer Service Page

Even though you don't have to order the fulfillment of your product personally, you need to make sure that the customer has a place for grievance redressal. A couple of pages that you must create include a page for exchange and refund policies, contact, FAQs, shipping and tracking, and size charts. Carefully go through all the different procedures that the print company has about handling issues and complaints. Your policies will depend on their policies. For instance, if the print fulfillment company needs photographic evidence to deal with a problem, then make sure that your store policy does too. Try to be as comprehensive as you can when you create these pages. The more detailed the information you provide, the fewer problems you will run into.

## Step 5: Design

It is a fun part of the business operation. Now is the time to unleash all your creative ideas about t-shirt designs and designing. Go through the design guidelines of the printing company before you start to design the t-shirts. They tend to offer different templates so that you can place and design the t-shirts properly. It will be a waste of time and effort if you design something that the fulfillment company cannot print. There are different guidelines that the printing company will provide regarding saving and uploading files. You must pay attention to the various specifications they provide. You can use tools like Adobe Illustrator, Canva, or even Snappa to design t-shirts.

### Step 6: Create a Mockup

Now is the time to test your design. You must know how the finished product will look, don't you? Well, create a mockup of your design, and you can see for yourself. It will also help you to make any necessary changes. You need to remember that the mockup will closely resemble the finished product you offer your customers. Make sure that it is of good quality and is something that the customers will want to purchase.

### Step 7: Upload Your Designs

Carefully follow the instructions that the fulfillment company provides when you upload your designs and link them to each of the individual listings. You can set printing options as well as the sizes here. If you have multiple options or designs you want to sell, then you must do the same for each item. You can upload a mockup of the design.

### Step 8: Order Samples

It is another epic milestone for your business. It is a critical step, and the success of your t-shirt designing business will depend on the print fulfillment company's ability to deliver. Place an order for a sample and see how it is delivered. Pay attention to the quality of the t-shirt, the quality of the print, the delivery time, shipping time, and packaging. If something doesn't meet your expectations, you can always change it quickly. You will probably have to go through a couple of samples until you find one that fits your needs.

**Step 9: Product Pricing**

Now that you have everything ready, the next step is to price your t-shirts. Not just that, you need to write product descriptions as well. How do you price your products? The price will depend on the cost that the fulfillment company will charge you. A print fulfillment company makes a profit on the base fee that they charge per product. Look at this example for the price of a t-shirt: $10 (t-shirt) + $5 (shipping)= $15. You can add up your markup cost to the base price of the fulfillment company. If you want to make a profit of $10, you can sell the t-shirts at $20 and add another $5 for shipping. The base price of the t-shirts will depend on the brand and the quality of the material. So, you need to try out a couple of pricing policies before you find one that meets your requirements. Once you have a price in mind, you must write the product descriptions. Try to make the descriptions seem as interesting as possible. For instance, you can write about your inspiration for the idea, or even something quirky about the t-shirt. Or you can advise on how you can style the t-shirt. Provide information about the material and sizing. Sizing is an essential aspect, and you must be careful about it. Mention the cut and fit of the t-shirt as well. Since the customer cannot see the physical product in real time, you must make your description as detailed as possible.

Well, now all you need to do is get your store up and running!

# Chapter 12: Social Media Marketing

## Best Platforms

There are few people who have not heard of the likes of Facebook and Twitter but there are other social media platforms that, used in the right way, can be very effective in your marketing campaign. We are going to look at the top social media platforms and how they can help your social media marketing campaign.

## Facebook

Facebook is undeniably the most popular social media platform there are these days and it has over 1.2 billion active users. It is a great advertising platform for all businesses since it offers both free and paid advertising options. It also offers you the opportunity to create a business profile, and you must use it to keep in touch with your target audience. You can also use this platform to build your list of subscribers and engage with your audience directly. The advertising system on Facebook is PPC (Pay per click) and it allows you to direct specific ads at your target audience.

## Twitter

It is a microblogging and networking platform that has over 200 million active users. It is quite popular amongst celebrities, entrepreneurs, and other businesses to provide regular updates. The regular updates are known as Tweets and a tweet cannot exceed 140 characters. This restriction on text certainly makes it quite compatible with the SMS system. You can create a Twitter profile for your business and use it to attract followers.

## Instagram

Instagram is an extremely popular social media site these days and is meant for sharing visual media. You can share a photo as well as video media on this platform. Instagram boasts over 150 million active monthly users. It is a great platform for all businesses that like to engage with their audience through visual media. A business can post photos and videos of their products, behind-the-scenes glimpses, and even use it as a promotional tool.

## YouTube

YouTube has grown into an influential social media platform. What started out as a fun medium of introducing the world to three-dimensional interaction has now turned into a powerful tool of marketing. Just like every other social media channel, the secret to success is getting a following or audience to broadcast your videos to. The more views you get, the more popular your videos will be and the greater success you will have in ranking highly in search results. People can comment on your videos and even share them across other platforms like Twitter, Google+, or Facebook.

## Tips

If you have decided that social media marketing is the way to go for your business, you will find these tips invaluable.

## Select the Right Platform

If you want to use social media to promote your business, then you need to select the perfect platform for this purpose. You need to opt for a platform that a majority of your target audience uses actively. It doesn't make sense to promote your business on a platform that your target audience hardly uses. Also, it isn't a good idea to use all the platforms of social media to promote your business. Not only is it difficult to do so, but it can be quite expensive in terms of time and funds spent.

## Always Evaluate

There is a lot of data available these days about performance metrics, your audience, and your business. You need to evaluate all the data. There are some social media platforms that provide analytical tools that you can use for this purpose. Apart from this, there are several third-party apps and services that you can use to analyze the data you collect. You can use metrics like views, shares, and comments on your social media profile to design your marketing campaign. Social media marketing is about increasing the reach of your business.

## Timing

The content that you post is critical, but that's not what social marketing is all about. You need to work to increase the interaction your audience has with your posts. So, it is important that you time your posts. You need to post at a time when you know that a majority of your audience will be active on your chosen platform.

## Establish Connections

A common mistake that a lot of social media marketers make is that they don't interact with their audience. You need to interact with your audience and engage them. You cannot build a loyal customer base for your business if you don't talk to your audience. The audience needs to know that they are communicating with a human being and not an automated bot. Don't engage in a monologue, instead, strive to strike a dialogue with your audience.

## Visual route

Large blocks of text can be rather off-putting. So, instead, go the visual route and use lots of images, videos, and infographics in your marketing campaign. All these visual means are not only appealing but are easy to understand as well. Even if you write a brilliant essay, no one has the time or patience to go through it.

## Make the Platforms Unique

A person who is following your business on one platform might follow you on some other platform as well. So, while you repurpose your content, make sure that you aren't merely posting the same content everywhere. For instance, the content that you use on FB can be repurposed for your campaign on YouTube or Snapchat. You can use similar content, but don't make it repetitive. Not just that, you need to customize the content according to the platform that you choose to use. The images that you use on Snapchat cannot be repurposed for Instagram.

## Be Appreciative

You need to understand that everyone likes to be acknowledged. In fact, it is a basic human desire to feel appreciated. So, you can offer rewards to your followers for subscribing or following you. It can be something as simple as a thank you or even a special discount. People need to know that their support is appreciated. You need to make it worthwhile for your audience to follow you.

## Be Personable

Social media is certainly a more relaxed manner of marketing than conventional marketing methods. It doesn't mean that you completely forego all sorts of professionalism. You need to be personable on social media for others to like you. Try to engage in some harmless and engaging banter with your audience. You can ask them for their opinions on certain topics and provide them some personal information that will lend a human touch to your business.

### Social Media Manager

If you think you cannot handle a social media marketing campaign, then you can always hire a social media manager who will do the work for you. It is always a good idea to reach out for additional help when you know that you cannot do something by yourself.

### Walk Away

If you feel that a certain aspect of the social media marketing strategy is not working for your business, then ditch it. It is quite likely that everything will not work out favorably for you. If something doesn't work, cut your losses, and ditch it. Instead, you can focus all your resources on a campaign that seems to be working well for you.

### Network

Use social media to not just network with your audience, but other businesses in your niche or industry. It is always a good idea to build relations with other businesses (not your direct competitors).

### It Is Not Just a Slice of the Marketing Pie

Most marketers tend to believe that social media is nothing but another platform that businesses and brands can use to distribute their message. Yes, social media does help you with this, but that's not the sole purpose it serves. If you keep using your social media to only post promotional content, then you will certainly end up as a social media road kill. You need to use your social media accounts to familiarize the account with your brand and use it to increase your reach. For instance, if your business has a profile on Instagram and all that you do on it is give sales pitches, you will quickly lose followers and it will not do you any good.

## Social-Media Experts

It is always a good idea to hire a social media expert whenever you need some additional help. One thing that you need to be wary of is the so-called social media experts who are all talk. A lot of these people can certainly talk the talk but cannot walk the walk. If someone claims to be an expert or an authority on social media, then they need to support such claims with sufficient evidence and quantifiable results. If you think that you can manage your social media campaigns by yourself, then please go ahead and do so.

## Some Things Never Change

In the recent past, the world of marketing has undergone tremendous change. It doesn't mean that the old-fashioned rules about communication, PR and marketing don't hold true anymore. These basic ethics can never go out of fashion. It is imperative to understand your target audience; the value you can add to their lives and the purpose your business serves. You need to consider all this if you want to develop an effective marketing strategy. Also, you must never forget that social media is only a small part of your marketing strategy and not the entire strategy. So, don't stray away from these values when you consider the option of social media marketing. If you want your social media marketing campaign to be successful, then there are various elements that need to come together perfectly. All the elements of your campaign need to be in a symbiotic relation with each other. Social media is just one element of your campaign and you need to make all other elements work together seamlessly. You must use the traditional methods of marketing and try to incorporate social media marketing into them.

# Chapter 13: Affiliate Marketing

It can be quite difficult to sell a product or market a service, especially when you cannot reach your target audience. At times, you need different means to sell your products, or you might need to make some extra money. In such cases, you must opt for affiliate marketing. In affiliate marketing, a vendor sells their products or services with the help of an affiliate. The affiliate will help to market and promote the products to potential customers. It will help the vendor make a sale, and the vendor will pay the affiliate a certain fee for the effort they make.

Affiliate marketing is quite prevalent these days. It can be something as simple as writing a review for a product or service on a social media platform. In this section, you will learn about selecting an affiliate program and earning money from affiliate marketing.

## Selecting an Affiliate Program

## Avoid Paid-For Programs

A simple Google search for "affiliate marketing programs" will provide you tens of thousands of hits. Some companies will ask you to pay a fee to join their program. All the fancy downloadable applications include well-thought-out payment plans. Not just that, they even try to hype their fee by giving you a so-called "discount" on their fee or other "special plans" to lure unsuspecting users. If you ever come across such a website, you must run in the opposite direction.

When you search for affiliate programs, trust your gut. An affiliate program will not provide you a commission unless you make a sale. Remember that they need your help to make the deal. So, why must you pay the company to provide them with your advice? It doesn't make any sense, does it? Steer clear such websites that ask you to pay a fee to join their affiliate program. Don't ever give out your credit card details and you certainly must not make an online banking transaction on a website that seems spurious.

## Check the Business

Any affiliate program you wish to join must add value to your site. It must be something that visitors to your site will find useful. If you want to increase website traffic, then you must look for those affiliates that go well with your website. You have complete autonomy to select the affiliate you want to work with. You can check a couple of sites or blogs to see the kind of affiliates they host. Once you know what you are looking for, you can contact them yourself.

Make a list of businesses that you would like to associate yourself with. Once you do this, the next thing you must do is check if the website is user-friendly. Try to think about the affiliate program from the perspective of your audience. Will they want to click on the link? If so, then how easy is it to complete a transaction? You must believe in the website before you decide to endorse it to your users. You can place an order on the site and see the process for yourself. You can lose your audience if you provide them with links that seem out of place or unnecessary to them.

## The Terms and Conditions

If you are happy and confident about the company or business you select, you must go through their terms and conditions. You must be aware of all their terms and conditions before you decide to get involved with them. Understand how the program works, the commission you will receive, as well as the terms of the contract. Understand the payment mechanism. You can even set a commission rate for yourself. Money is an essential aspect of affiliate marketing. After all, you are using your audience base to improve the sales of the company. You deserve a good commission for the effort you make. Carefully read through the clauses regarding rights and obligations, along with termination clauses. Accept it only when you feel that it is worth your while.

### Earn from Affiliate Marketing

If you want to build a passive stream of income for yourself from affiliate marketing, it will take considerable time and effort. Don't expect to be successful overnight. Here are a couple of things that will help you to increase your earnings from affiliate marketing:

### Build Your Website Traffic

Affiliate marketing thrives on people's interest in clicking on links to products that catch their eye. But who are these "people"? Well, these are people who will visit your blog or website to read what you have written. So, in order to lure these people, you have to make your blog or site as interesting as possible. It is fine to go all out and decorate it as much as you like. But make sure you keep with the theme otherwise people will only visit to mock your blog. You need to have a good readership or audience base if you want to venture into affiliate marketing. If you don't have a readership, who will you be marketing to? Not just that, why will a company or a business even want to make use of your services if you don't have a good reach? Spend some time building your PR. It will help in increasing your reach and the greater the number of people who are aware of you and your services, the higher your chances of being successful in affiliate marketing. So, you obviously must not create your own website tonight and join an affiliate marketing program tomorrow. It doesn't make any sense.

**A Good Product or Service Will Do**

Newcomers to the system often make the mistake of peppering their site or sites with lots of different things, imagining that people are likely to buy more because they have more choice. You are not a store – you don't have to offer your customers choice, because they did not land on your site with a purchase in mind. Think of yourself as a pop-up store to promote one product as opposed to a super market that offers a lot of choices.

It is always the power of suggestion that works on a majority of customers. They will take a liking to something if you tell them that you are offering them the same product that you have personally tested and liked yourself. If you have put up just one product or service and the website is offering it at the best price in the market then even if the person has left your site to do a quick price comparison, he or she is sure to return back to yours to click on the ad. Also, focusing on a single product or business makes it easier to make keywords work for you.

**Content Is Crucial**

Viewers go to websites to be informed or entertained – often both at the same time. So, make sure you have plenty of content structured around the products or business you are promoting. Another point to remember is that search engines can tell whether there's quality content on your site, and will rank it higher as a result. That means more visitors and hopefully more sales. You need to work on SEO as well. It refers to search engine optimization. You can improve your online visibility by increasing your SEO as well. You must select all the top words or keywords from your blog or website, that is most likely going to be typed by people. But remember just a good SEO description will not do the trick and you need to have good content as well.

The content you are offering must not just be interesting; it needs to be engaging as well. Also, make sure that the content consists of different topics and not just one genre. You can attract and improve your audience base by doing this. You must also make sure that the quality of the content you are offering stays the same throughout. Viewers will stop visiting your website or blog if your content isn't of good quality. Don't bombard your users with too many links and promos. The subtle power of suggestion works better than flooding them with affiliate links.

**Promote Your Site**

Without proper promotion, how are you going to get the word about your website out there? There are only so many friends that will click on your links in order for you to land a major gig. Start by listing your site on search engines, write press releases to be distributed online, and promote your site on forums in your niche and social media. If you have a friend whose blog is extremely popular then you can ask him or her to subtly promote yours on theirs. Ideally, choose another blog that speaks on topics like yours or something along the same lines. Make use of various social media platforms for increasing your website's popularity as well. Work on building an army of followers, but don't ever consider buying them.

Followers who are bought aren't going to go to your website and click on the affiliate links – they simply provide the false illusion that your social media account is more popular than it is. You might think that you are popular, but once that bubble bursts, you might be extremely disappointed. So, try to find a diverse group who will not lose interest in your writing and don't force anyone or buy anyone for the job. You cannot cheat your readers or your marketing partners. Remember, you will reap what you sow, and so it is best that you remain as honest and trustworthy as possible.

## Don't Be Invisible or Anonymous

A golden rule of online marketing is that you must not be invisible or anonymous. You must have confidence in who you are and what you do. If you don't have the necessary self-confidence, then don't expect things will work in your favor. Think of a scenario where you have to address an important crowd consisting of your potential clients and you don't have the confidence to reveal your true identity.

Well, that certainly must not work out well for you. It might be quite easy to hide behind an alias on the web, but that doesn't mean you must do this. If you want to build your online credibility, then you must not hide behind a really cool username. Instead, you must focus on making your true persona known to as many people as you possibly can. If you want to use a pen name, and then make sure that your real name is included in brackets beside the pen name. Make sure you write out your full name including initials, as there can be many others with the same name as you.

People need to know they can contact you with questions, and that they will get an answer from a real person. They might also ask for a genuine photograph just to be sure of who the other person is. If they aren't confident about your blog or website, then it is highly unlikely that they will even want to click on any affiliate links that you advertised on your blog. Make sure that you reply to any queries that a user posts. You can't trust a client who must not reply to your queries, will you? Well, the same applies to other users as well. People will be wary of doubting a person who doesn't even reveal his or her true identity.

Affiliate is a wonderful way in which you can monetize your website, blog, or any other online portal, and earn money online. It helps you to create a perpetual stream of passive income. However, it is not just about signing up and getting started. You need to check what is on offer and be certain that you are happy and comfortable with the particular service or product that you are promoting. Remember, you need to put in considerable time and effort if you want to earn good returns.

Don't start flooding your web space with lots of affiliate links for various products. It is likely that your readers will be put off because they will feel like they are being spammed. So, try to restrict the number of links you provide your readers. Make use of a soft sell approach, create good content for engaging your readers, and then you can gradually steer them towards affiliate links. When done properly, affiliate marketing can be quite enjoyable and lucrative. However, it does take some time for building up your online presence as well as trust, so don't think about rushing things. Take time for getting everything right, and soon you can start enjoying a steady stream of passive income through affiliate marketing.

# Chapter 14: Impulse Buying

Impulsive buyers are buyers who make a purchase on a whim and without any planning. A purchase that is made on the spur of the moment that provides instant gratification to the buyer is an impulse purchase. Impulsive buyers can be a boon for any business. As a drop shipper, you will need to work hard to encourage impulsive buying. In this section, you will learn about a couple of ways in which you can promote impulsive buying.

## Conditional Free Shipping

Free shipping can be quite compelling and can help increase the value of an online shopper. You can use this to your advantage while you structure your shipping offer. Calculate the average order value and make it around $20-$50 and you can offer free shipping if a purchase is between these amounts. Take a moment and think about it. If you want to buy something online and your purchase amounts to $40, but the shipping charges are $5, then you will hesitate for a moment about the purchase. Instead, you can offer conditional free shipping if the shopper makes a purchase for a specific amount like $40. You can even encourage shoppers by coming up with a couple of suggestions in the specific price group during checkout to encourage them to meet the conditional limit.

## Sales and Promotions

Incentives, as well as special pricing, will help increase impulse purchases. You can use a sale or promotion to encourage customers to make a purchase just like you use free shipping. Often, in a physical retail outlet, low-priced items are the ones that are often purchased. Similarly, you can come up with a sale to drive impulse purchases.

## Mobile Optimization

The main reason that encourages customers to impulsively buy something is that online shopping is quick and easy. So, if someone decides to make an unplanned purchase, then a slow and tedious buying process will be off putting. You need to ensure that your website is streamlined and is optimized for mobile usage. You can even develop a mobile app to help you with this.

## Web Design

There is a direct relationship that exists between impulse buying and the quality of the website. You need to make sure that your website design is of high-quality. The website needs to look appealing to a buyer and it is quite likely that the customer will end up buying something.

# Chapter 15: Product Listings

Product listing refers to the listing of all the products in a particular category and is also known as category pages. Usually, customers tend to review product listings before selecting a specific product.

In this section, you will learn about product listings on your website.

## Information

A common question that a lot of business owners have while listing their products is what information must be displayed for individual products on the listing page and what must be displayed on the product page? The two important things that you must consider while determining the answer to this question are: The category page must always include all the possible information that a customer will need to choose between the available products. According to the customer segment, this information will vary. So, you need to have all the necessary information regarding the style, budget, or any other unique feature of the product to help the customer make a decision. The information that you provide on the category pages for the products needs to be precise and you must avoid unnecessary information. Try to limit the content on this page since your main idea is to fit as many products on a page as you possibly can. It helps make the list more usable for the customer. In fact, it is better to not include any information that isn't necessary for selection; instead, you can use the information on the product page.

## Photos, Icons and Graphics

To make your category page appealing, you need to include high-quality photos of products. A picture is certainly worth a thousand words, so choose pictures wisely to avoid the need for extra product information. While including the product information, try not to overwhelm the viewer. The photos you use must be sized properly so that you can display a lot of products on each page. Also, the images you use must not be flashy and must not be airbrushed. You will need to deal with a lot of unhappy customers if you use images that make the product appear better than they are.

You can even use icons for your store, provided that they are all structured around a single type of product, meaning much of the product information you include is similar for all products. If that's the case, then you can create a system of icons that you can use.

## Number of Products per Row

The number of products that you want to list in a row will depend on the information that needs to be displayed about a product. It essentially depends on the different qualities that a customer might want to use to select something along with whether the customer finds those qualities desirable or not. The usual practice is to list one product in a row and is often wasteful. So, list only one product per row if you think the information you are providing is absolutely necessary. There are stores that list five or even six products in a row, but this is not desirable. When you list so many products in a row, the product image tends to become too small and the scope to display information is drastically reduced. You need to strike a balance between these two extremes. Ideally, it is good practice to display about two or three images in a row.

## Number of Products per Page

The number of products that you list on a category page is the next aspect of product listing you need to decide. It is convenient to scroll through a page instead of waiting for the next page to load. So, you can include as many products as you want on a page. Usually, websites display around ten products per page, even if they list only one product per row. Until a couple of years ago, businesses used to avoid displaying a lot of products on a page because of the long download time. A lot of products meant a lot of pictures and it meant the page used to take a while to download. Well, now all this is a concern of the past. With the introduction of high-speed Internet connections, it hardly takes a fraction of a second to display a webpage. Ideally, try to stick to less than 50 products per page.

A lot of category pages have a dropdown list that allows the customer to select the number of products that they will want to view at any given time. The Items per Page dropdown menu must list the multiples of the number of products that are displayed in a row. For instance, if you decide to display 5 images in a row, then the Items per Page numbers must include 10, 20, 30, 40, and so on.

## Sorting

You must always provide your customers with the option of sorting the product display on the page. When you do this, it makes the category pages quite effective and easy to navigate. Not just that, it also helps the customers view the products that meet their specific criteria. Sorting options must always be based on the information or the features that will be relevant to your target audience.

When the customer has the option to sort the products according to a specific quality they are looking for, it is easier to narrow down the number of appropriate items and also requires less filtering. It is a good idea to provide different sorting options to your customers apart from the default sort order.

There are two reasons why the default sort order is important. The first reason is that, even though a customer can change this order, most customers tend to use this default setting. The second reason is that you can control the default sort order and it is similar to a list of recommendations.

# Chapter 16: Scaling

In this section, you will learn about the ways in which you can scale your dropshipping business.

A lot of people simply assume that you need to use only Facebook ads for scaling up your business. In fact, there are different ways in which you can do this. Your odds of succeeding at scaling your business are directly proportional to the number of scaling strategies that you have in your marketing arsenal. You can scale your business in the following ways:

Sales teams include cold calling and cold emailing procedures. You can use Facebook lookalike audiences, similar audiences on Google, using different types of advertising platforms, you can recruit a team of affiliate marketers to promote your business, work with top influencers on social media, you can also increase your budget for advertising in small installments, duplicate winning ad campaigns to target the same or new audience, and franchising or creating duplicates of your store in different places.

The one thing that is common for all these methods is that they will enable you to obtain new customers and increase your sales in a predictable manner. There is no upper limit to the number of customers you can obtain from these methods and they will certainly increase your sales too. So, how else can you scale your business?

You can scale your business horizontally, which means that you will be going wider instead of deeper. For instance, let us assume that you spend about $5 per day for a Facebook ad and that specific ad set is doing well. One way in which you can scale the ad set is to increase your daily budget in small installments. So, instead of finding a new audience you will just increase your ad budget to an ad set that is doing well. This is an example of scaling vertically. Alternatively, you can duplicate this ad set, or you can create multiple ads that are similar and try to target new pages on Facebook that you haven't explored yet. When you do this, you are scaling wider instead of vertically.

The best way to scale up your dropshipping business horizontally is to use the franchising technique. It is a good method to scale your dropshipping business. No, it isn't about KFC or Starbucks outlets, but you can use a similar method to scale your existing dropshipping business. Instead of trying to expand your customer base in one country, you will need to duplicate the entire store in a new country and target a newer audience.

For instance, if you have a dropshipping store in the USA, you can use Facebook ads to target your ideal customers. Once this store starts to do well, you decide to duplicate this store in another country, like Spain, you need someone to translate your English store and all the ads into Spanish. You will also need to hire someone to take care of customer support. Once you do this, your store will start to do well in Spain as well. This is an example of scaling your business horizontally. You can expand your business to as many countries as you want to and possibly can. Make sure that you have someone around who can communicate fluently in the local language of the country you decide to set up a store in for customer support. If not, you can always hire help for this purpose. You might or might not want to scale up your business with multiple stores. So, what can you do in such a situation? Can you keep your dropshipping store and use it to target a worldwide audience? You most certainly can do this. In fact, this is the second method in which you can scale up your business.

It is less efficient than duplicating the store and translating all ads and content.

The greater number of stores you have, the Facebook ads and the marketing tools you use are tailored for the specific audience you are targeting. In such a case, the rate of conversion is also higher. For instance, if you have a store in Germany or Spain, then people have the option of shopping in their native language and the currency they use. The storefront is tailor-made to suit their needs and requirements. It doesn't mean that you will not have any customers if your global store is in English and the currency you use is USD. If someone doesn't like to pay in USD, is suspicious of purchasing something from a foreign store or doesn't speak English, then such a customer will not make a purchase.

So, which of these strategies can you use to scale your store? The answer to this question depends on the number of countries you plan to target. If your store is successful in one language and you are fluent in another language as well, then it is a good idea to duplicate the store. The one thing that you need to keep in mind is that duplication of a store takes a lot of work and, therefore, the number of countries you can target is quite low. You can also get higher rates of conversion, but the potential of scalability reduces.

On the other hand, if you have one global store, then you can duplicate your best-performing ad sets and target various other countries, but the conversion rate will be lower. But it does offer you the opportunity to scale wider.
The best way to decide which of these methods will work for your business is to try them! Start with a global store and then see how things work for you.

# Chapter 17: Passive Income and Virtual Assistants

If you want a source of passive income, then it is important that you outsource certain daily tasks. In this section, you will learn about how, when, and why you must outsource. Apart from this, you will also learn to hire, train, and manage remote virtual assistants.

## Why Do You Need a Virtual Assistant?

The first reason why you need a virtual assistant (VA) is that time is an invaluable asset and in business time is money. For instance, if you have to take care of several businesses or have to juggle between a regular job and dropshipping, then a VA will make your life easier. If you spend all your time handing complaints, responding to emails, dealing with service requests, or even fulfilling orders, you will not have time left to manage and grow your businesses. A virtual assistant will take care of all the repetitive tasks that don't require your presence. It will help you optimally utilize your valuable time.

## When to Hire a VA?

Don't hire a virtual assistant in the beginning. You will need a VA once your business starts to process over 10-15 orders per day. In the beginning, you can take care of all the aspects of your dropshipping business like market research, customer support and everything else involved. In fact, it is a good idea that you do all this by yourself initially. It will give you an idea of how things work and what you need to do. In fact, you must do all of this occasionally even after you hire a VA.

## What Positions Are VA's Suitable For?

The first VA you decide to hire needs to handle a couple of aspects of the dropshipping business like handling business communication (responding to emails, comments, and messages), customer support and order fulfillment. You need to find a VA who has a good knowledge of the dropshipping business. Once your store starts to grow and the orders, support requests, and business communication increase, you can hire other virtual assistants according to the work. The second VA you hire can take care of all aspects of business communication and can eventually start doing all the market research and add new products to the product list. In this manner, you can edit the description of all the new products and launch your ads. All this saves time. You don't need to hire any full-time virtual assistants and you need them for about 1-3 hours per day.

Delegation might not be something that comes to you naturally. If you want to automate your business and convert your dropshipping enterprise into a passive stream of income, then you need virtual assistants. In this section, you will learn about the different ways in which you can hire a virtual assistant and the tasks that you can delegate.

## Tasks You Can Outsource

The dropshipping business is quite lucrative and it provides you an opportunity to be your own boss. There are various perks of dropshipping business and you can work on it while holding onto a regular 9-5 job. Initially, everything might seem quite peachy and exciting, but what will happen when you try to expand your business? The workload will increase and the number of things you need to handle will increase as well. All this can be quite overwhelming. What is the solution to this problem? The solution is quite simple, and it is outsourcing.

Outsourcing is the process of making someone outside your business handle certain aspects of your business instead of doing it in-house. The good news is that there are several aspects of the dropshipping business that you can outsource to free up your time and reduce your workload.

You can pretty much outsource all the aspects of your business, but here are the top tasks that you can easily outsource:

## Market Research

The first task that you can outsource is market research. It takes a lot of time and effort to research the items that will prove to be profitable for your business.

Market research is an ongoing process and you cannot stop doing this once you start your business. You must not only look for newer products, but you must check your competition and evaluate the different platforms that you can use for your business.

## Product Listing

Another task that can take up a lot of time is product listing on your store. You can outsource this responsibility and, in fact, you can hire a professional to do this work for you.

## Data Entry

Let us face it, data entry is a simple task, but it is quite time consuming and cumbersome. Data entry is an important part of your research and you can outsource it these days.

## Customer Service

Ideally, it is a good idea to handle customer service by yourself. As a business owner, it makes more sense to outsource this task to someone else. Instead of spending all your time answering queries, responding to mails, dealing with returns, and providing assistance to customers, you can concentrate on something else.

## Content

Good content is critical for your business. You need content for not just your website, but for product descriptions, social media posts, and even any other blog posts you want to make. It can take up a lot of your precious time. You can instead hire a copywriter to help you create exceptional content.

## Optimize Product Titles

Another task that you can take off your plate is optimizing product listings. You can hire a freelancer to do this work for you.

There are other tasks that you can outsource like building and maintaining your website, emailing potential clients and suppliers, managing your schedule, HTML templates for product listings, and graphics for your images and logos too.

So, where can you find reliable workers for all this? The three best websites that you can hire trustworthy freelancers from are Upwork, Freelancer, and Fiverr.

## Hire a Virtual Assistant

## Post a Job

The best way to find a VA is through your network and ask for referrals. It is always better to look for people who come with a recommendation. You can look for VA's by posting an ad for the same on different platforms like Slack, LinkedIn or even Facebook. Social media is the best way to reach anyone. Apart from this, there are different platforms that you can use to find a virtual assistant like Upwork, Zirtual, and UAssistMe. You can also use freelance marketplaces like Guru, TaskPigeon, PeoplePerHour, and Freelancer to find a VA for your dropshipping business.

Whenever you post an ad, you need to make sure that it is precise, engaging, and includes the key phrases that a potential VA might look for like customer service assistant or business communications assistant. To save time in the weeding out process and qualifying applicants, you can as, the applicants, give the answer to a random question in the first line of the reply. If you do this, it will help to review only those applicants you took the time that read the job post thoroughly. The job description you give in the post is quite important when you are trying to attract the right candidates. You need to include a couple of details like business volume, the apps, and the platforms your business uses any language requirements, and the specific tasks they will need to perform.

**Shortlist and Interview**

Once you go through all the applications you receive, the next step is to shortlist the candidates and schedule interviews. You can use any of the video platforms like Skype or Google Hangouts to conduct the interview. The interview must not last for longer than 30 minutes and you need to prepare a questionnaire. You need to include certain vital questions to determine the skillset and the mindset of the applicant. You must remember that you can always teach a person a new skill, but you cannot change their mindset.

The questions you can ask the applicant are:

What do they enjoy doing? What are the skills that you want them to learn or perfect? What are their strengths? What made them respond to your ad? What do they usually do in their free time? What is their educational background?

Once you are certain that you have chosen the perfect candidate, the next step is to discuss payment. Usually, virtual assistants get paid anywhere between $5 per hour to $25 per hour. If you decide to hire someone from Upwork you can set up an hourly contract with them and the payment will be directly wired to them according to the number of hours they clock.

It is a good idea to give your VA a trial task to observe their skills. If the VA passes the test, you can offer a trial period for two weeks to test the VA's capabilities. If things go well, then you can start delegating manual tasks to the VA.

## On-Boarding

Usually, candidates tend to exit during the trial period. So, it is a good idea to get the two VA's onboard simultaneously. You will have the opportunity to witness whether they are as good as they claim to be or not. The best-case scenario is that you might end up with two good VA's in the end.

## Guidelines

You need to create a training manual as well as written guidelines for the on-boarding process. You can use certain videos or recordings to go together with the written guides to train your VA. If you are training a VA, make sure that you record the training sessions and you can use them to train future VA's.

## Training

There are different online resources that you can use to train remote virtual assistants to do specific tasks or use specific tools. For instance, HubSpot Academy is one of the best online places to learn about things like content creation, web designing, email marketing, and the like. HubSpot offers several engaging and detailed online classes to learn about the different aspects of running an online business. Another resource that you can use to teach your VA's about SEO is Moz's Beginner's Guide to SEO. SEO increases the online visibility of your business and is an important area that you need to concentrate on. Use the above-mentioned tool to teach your VA's about how they can research for keywords, learn the way search engines work, and also learn to measure and track the success rate of their keywords.

If you use any form of paid advertising and you want to teach your VA to manage it, then you can use WordStream's PPC University to get them better acquainted with paid advertising campaigns. This is a great place for anyone who wants to learn about CTR, CPC, negative keywords, split-advertisement testing, and all other aspects of PPC advertising. A couple of other platforms you can use to train your Virtual Assistants are Social Media Quickstarter, CodeAcademy, and Canva's Design School.

**Management**

Your job doesn't end once you hire a VA. You not only need to ensure that the work goes smoothly, but you also need to make sure that you nurture this relationship. It is your responsibility to make sure the VA is satisfied with his or her job profile and is learning things that will benefit the VA as well as your business. If your VA starts to lose interest or the relationship becomes stale, then it is likely that the VA will quit, to ensure that this doesn't happen, you need to effectively manage the virtual assistants. You can ask the VA to send you a weekly update about all the things that they have achieved and the tasks they have completed. You can also schedule weekly calls and go over the projects or tasks you want the VA to perform and discuss those areas in which they excelled and the ones you want them to improve on. The greater the trust that you establish, the lesser time is necessary to supervise and motivate your VA to work.

Ideally, you need to develop a working relationship where the VA works independently. Doing this will not only help in the growth of the VA, but it will also make you comfortable with delegating complex responsibilities.

## Communication

There are different apps and platforms that you can use to communicate with your VA. Here are a couple of apps and platforms that you can use for this purpose.

If you want to create projects and then assign them to a group of VA's or a team, then you can use Asana. Slack is an amazing platform for not just communication but even collaboration for all work-related tasks. If you want to create to-do lists, then Trello is the app for you. Use YouCanBook.Me for scheduling meetings in a simple and quick manner. If you want to text and chat for free while on the go, then WhatsApp must be your go-to app. Use Skype or Google Hangouts for making video calls. If you want to share files or any other documents, then Google Drive is the best option available these days.

## Delegation

Delegation isn't something that comes easy for a lot of people. In fact, it can be quite difficult for a business owner to start delegating tasks. It can be difficult to entrust your business responsibilities to someone else, especially when you have built everything up from scratch. If you want to expand or build a team for yourself, then delegation is quite important. You can free up your valuable time to concentrate on the important aspects of the business with the help of a VA. You need to create a working system that not only works for you but works for your VA as well. The goal is to free up your time so that you can concentrate on the things that matter. It might take you a while until you find someone who you trust and get along well with. Hiring a VA will certainly be worth all the hassle that you go through.

## Investment

You need to understand that your VA is an investment and you must treat the VA accordingly. VA is an investment of your time as well as money. You need to consider that your business might last longer than you. If you want to build a personal brand, then you need a VA to help you along the way. Take a moment to think about some strong personal brands present in the business. Names like Steve Jobs and Richard Branson come up quite often. Even though Steve Jobs is long gone, his reputation lives on and will live for a long time. It isn't just Jobs, but even Branson's reputation will outlive him as well. These leaders have a persona that oozes originality, creativity, and something else that makes them quite special.

If you hire a VA, then you will have some assistance while building your personal brand. In fact, think of hiring a VA as an investment on behalf of your business. You need to spend time to train and develop the VA so that they can generate ROI.

# Chapter 18: Advertising and Dropshipping

## Build Trust

The first thing you can do to advertise your dropshipping business is to build trust by adding customer reviews and testimonials to your website. First-time shoppers usually are skeptical about the quality of the products listed on the website. If you add some promising customer reviews, testimonials, and ratings to your business website, then it will build the visitor's trust. For instance, the drop shippers on AliExpress usually include a snapshot of the customer's feedback to their website. You can also use the reviews present on your supplier's store and add it to your website. If you want to expand your business, then it is a good idea to build your own set of testimonials, reviews, and ratings.

## Facebook Ads

There are more than two million active users on Facebook every month. You need to leverage the reach of this platform to advertise your dropshipping business. Facebook is a favorite platform for a lot of dropshipping businesses because of the diversity and the rich data it collects. It means that you can be as specific as you want while targeting ads on Facebook. Facebook ads offer a high degree of customizability. So, you can ensure that the right ads reach the desired audience.

You can customize these ads according to your budget, goal, and audience. You can also choose the format of the ads and select the places where you want to display the ad. The ads you run on Facebook can also be run on Messenger, Instagram, and Audience Network. If you want your Facebook ads campaign to be successful, then you need to invest in good video content. Video content is a great means to reach your potential audience and encourage them to interact with your brand. Video content is easier to understand and remember than textual content. Use Facebook ads to target all those on your contact list and your email list.

## Share Social Videos

Social videos make up for a significant part of the customer web traffic today. A dropshipping business can use video content to promote their business and their products. For instance, MakeBeauty usually shares sneak peeks of how-to videos on their social media accounts and later redirects the viewers to visit their webpage for complete instructional videos. It can be slightly challenging to create social videos, but it will be certainly worth your while. If you don't want to create new videos, then you can search for viral videos on popular sites and use them (don't forget to give due credit and seek permissions). You can then use call-to-action buttons on these videos to direct traffic to your dropshipping website.

## Retargeting

Most visitors don't usually make a purchase on their first visit. This can be a major hurdle for dropshipping websites since gaining traffic is not easy. In such a situation, you can use retargeting to recapture the visitor's attention. Retargeting is a simple marketing technique that targets previous visitors to your website who didn't take any action. It is your chance to capture an apparently lost opportunity. Once you retarget such visitors, it is quite likely that your sales will increase.

## Blog

You can start a blog to drive organic traffic to your business website. Blogs are frequently looked up to as sources of information. Blog marketing is a low-cost marketing strategy that will help you reach your target audience. The primary benefit of blog marketing for your business is that it helps you build your audience while generating more organic traffic to your business website. Another vital benefit of blog marketing is that it helps SEO results. SEO refers to Search Engine Optimization and is the process of enhancing the online visibility of your business. You can streamline your blog entries for SEO results.

## Identify Your Niche

You need to identify where your niche usually hangs around and try to join that group. A niche represents a community with a shared interest. All dropshipping businesses usually have a niche. You need to take advantage of this and make yourself a part of a niche and it offers a platform to connect with others who share a similar interest.

## Upsell and Cross-Sell

You can encourage shoppers to shop more with upselling and cross-selling marketing. A dropshipping business needs to maximize every transaction that's conducted. Usually, these two techniques are used synonymously, but there is a slight difference between the two. Both help increase the chances of impulsive buying and combining them into one strategy is a good idea.

# Conclusion

I want to thank you once again for choosing this book.

Dropshipping is a relatively new business model and is quite dynamic. There are different changes that keep taking place in this form of business. So, you need to make sure that you are always updated with the latest trends and business practices. In this book, you were provided with all the basic information that you need to start a dropshipping business. If you have any doubts, then you must refer to the concerned chapter in this book. If you are looking for more in-depth answers to your question, then don't hesitate to search for them on Google or YouTube. You need to soak up as much information as you can about this business model if you want to be a successful business owner.

Now, all that you need to do is get started. There is no time like the best to start. A wise old man once said, *"The best time to plant a tree was ten years ago and the next best time is now."*

The idea of starting a new business on your own might seem slightly daunting. All it takes is the first step to obtain the necessary momentum to keep going. So, don't be afraid and take the first step. If you put in the necessary hard work, dedicate sufficient time, and be patient, you will become a successful business owner.

An unfortunate fact is, most businesses fail in their first year, and only a few succeed. If you want to be a part of the successful minority, then you need the necessary motivation, strength, and determination to succeed. Failure must be considered as a stepping-stone to success. If you fail or run into obstacles, just pick yourself up, dust yourself off, and get back in the game. It is not easy, but when you succeed, there is nothing that can replace the high that success gives. Take everything in your stride and think of it as a learning experience. You can start your passive income journey today, and with the right mindset, it can be easy. The only thing that withholds you is your mindset. Remember that it is never too late to start, and you can always achieve something better for yourself. Don't give up on this feeling and keep it alive throughout your life!

Thank you and all the best!

# Description

It might seem quite tempting to select five passive income ideas to begin with. However, it is prudent to just stick to one. Every passive income business idea that you can think of requires time and focus on its growth. If you want to create a steady stream of passive income, then you must dedicate the necessary time and attention to your idea. It is better if you master one thing before you move onto another one. Passive income lives up to the hype it has in the market. However, to reach that stage, it takes plenty of time or money. Select an idea, create a plan, and then dedicate yourself to that program, and you certainly can rake in a handsome income.

## The Reason

Before you start, take a moment, and think about the idea that prompted you to opt for the particular stream, or option that you did. Is money the only reason that motivates you? The ability to generate passive income mainly depends on the audience. If the audience detects that it is all about making money for you and not serving their needs, then they won't be too kind to your business idea. Whenever you do something solely for money, you won't succeed. Your intentions need to go beyond acquiring the right bank balance if you want to achieve success. Unless you have a reason that provides you the drive to excel, you will not shine. Money is a byproduct of the desire that keeps you going. So, take some time and think about the reason and motivation for you to do so.

## A Lot of Time

The concept of overnight success is mythical, just like unicorns and leprechauns. You cannot expect to become a millionaire overnight. You have to put in all the necessary efforts and dedicate the time required to get there. Do you know that

Angry Birds was the 52nd game that Rovio designed? So, even when something might seem like an overnight success, it probably isn't. It takes a while for the business to kick off. However, don't expect results if you don't want to put in the necessary efforts.

**Forget About 100% Passive Income**

If you think that you can find an income stream that is 100% passive, then you are sadly mistaken. Let go of the thought that once you create a product, you can just bask in the sun and sip margaritas. Even with real estate rentals, you have to manage the property, or with the stock market, you have to continually keep an eye on the portfolio and handle it as well. Even with an online business, there isn't any such thing as 100% passive income. Passive income rests on the concept of the creation of business automation. However, if you want to keep yourself or your business automated, then keep the business going, then you need to put in a lot of time and effort. You cannot earn money without any effort.

**Find Your Ideal Market**

A lot of business ideas fail because people try to develop a product or build a business that caters to the needs of everyone. When you try to serve everyone around you, you cannot help anyone. You have to select a specialty and then build a niche or search for an existing one. Find a market that suits you or choose a market that you want to cater to. While you select a niche, your target audience takes into consideration your education and your interests as well. Your earnings are proportional to the audience base you serve.

CPSIA information can be obtained
at www.ICGtesting.com
Printed in the USA
LVHW011135191120
672145LV00015B/599